C000147985

Taming the Lion

100 Secret Strategies for Investing

Richard Farleigh

HARRIMAN HOUSE LTD

3A Penns Road
Petersfield
Hampshire
GU32 2EW
GREAT BRITAIN

Tel: +44 (0)1730 233870
Fax: +44 (0)1730 233880
Email: enquiries@harriman-house.com
Website: www.harriman-house.com

First published in Great Britain in 2005 by Harriman House Ltd.
Reprinted 2014

Copyright © Harriman House Ltd.

The right of Richard Farleigh to be identified as the author has been asserted
in accordance with the Copyright, Design and Patents Act 1988.

ISBN 978-0-857194-48-0

British Library Cataloguing in Publication Data
A CIP catalogue record for this book can be obtained from the British Library.

All rights reserved; no part of this publication may be reproduced, stored in a retrieval system,
or transmitted in any form or by any means, electronic, mechanical, photocopying, recording,
or otherwise without the prior written permission of the Publisher. This book may not be lent,
resold, hired out or otherwise disposed of by way of trade in any form of binding or cover
other than that in which it is published without the prior written consent of the Publisher.

No responsibility for loss occasioned to any person or corporate body acting or refraining to
act as a result of reading material in this book can be accepted by the Publisher, by the Author,
or by the employer of the Author.

For Camilla and the loves of our lives: "Toto", "Baba" and "Loulou".

With thanks to Janine Perrett, Peter Farleigh, Ross Thompson, Roy Travers, Robert Olson and of course, Marjorie Farleigh.

Contents

100 Secret Strategies for Investing

5 – Big Ideas

5.0 Markets are slow to react to structural influences

5.1 Look for the next big thing

5.2 Ignore obscure theories and observations

5.3 Only invest in the broad markets when they are in line with the prevailing economic environment

5.4 Be methodical - use a checklist to quantify and add rigour to a view

5.5 Buy stocks when economic growth is strong and inflation is weak

5.6 Buy bonds when inflation and economic growth are both weak

5.7 Buy commodities when inflation and economic growth are both strong

5.8 Few assets benefit when inflation is strong and economic growth is weak

5.9 You are unlikely to out-analyse the analysts

6 – Small Companies

6.0 Small companies offer more opportunities than large companies

6.1 The quality of a company's management is by far the most crucial factor in determining its success

6.2 Determining the fair valuation is more difficult with small companies

6.3 Clearly identify the comparative advantages

6.4 Be sure the business is sustainable

6.5 Good products don't always sell

6.6 Growth puts strains on small companies

6.7 Be sure of a route to exit and adequate cash resources

6.8 Shareholders can help unlisted companies

6.9 Be pragmatic with due diligence

9 – Market Timing

9.0   Combine fundamentals with price action

9.1   Ignore the noise in price movements

9.2   Don't be a hero - do not buy falling markets

9.3   Trade with the trend - wait for the trend before you enter the market

9.4   Add to winning trades, not losing trades

9.5   It is safe to be with the consensus

9.6   Do not use price targets or time limits

9.7   If the fundamentals have changed adjust the position accordingly

9.8   You will not get the high or the low

9.9   A powerful model shows probability is on your side

10 – Avoiding Temptation

10.0   Know when to stay out of the market

10.1   Identify what is difficult about the existing environment; it may change

10.2   Monitoring trends may alert you to opportunities you wouldn't normally find

10.3   With success, bank some profits

10.4   Negotiation is an art

10.5   The evolution of the con artist

10.6   Wealth preservation is not simple

10.7   Be sceptical of sophisticated retail products

10.8   Management and brokerage fees should be minimal in a passive portfolio

10.9   Follow these strategies and be part of the hedge fund (r)evolution

Richard and Camilla

Introduction

When I started my career in a Sydney investment bank in my early twenties, I did not believe that I could outperform the markets. As a former economist and a chess player, investment and trading just seemed to be a form of gambling. I had no idea how the markets could offer any opportunities.

Gradually, however, I came to believe that market prices are predictable, and within a few years I was running a trading desk dealing in hundreds of millions of dollars. Because I wanted a long and prosperous career, I developed a repeatable methodology which was based on observation and reasoning, not just on one-offs and luck.

I had many beliefs which went against conventional wisdom, some of which included:

- Markets tend to under-react, not overreact.
- Big, obvious ideas offer great opportunities.
- It is safe to invest with a consensus view.
- Contrarian trading is usually irrational.
- It is best to enter and exit the share market at the right times instead of always staying invested.
- Price trends are well known but under-utilised.
- Chartists are just astrologers.
- Investment and trading are increasingly similar.

Some things I simply tried to do better than other investors, these included being sure that I was chasing a genuine opportunity, managing my risks and coping with my losses.

I also developed some trading systems, which were still being used years after I left the bank.

As my trading results started to attract some attention, I was frequently asked to give presentations of my ideas to other professional traders. Question times often continued throughout dinner and in the bar. I learnt a lot from the feedback during these sessions. Like me, others were interested in an approach to investing which was based on first principles. I found that anecdotes were the best way to make a point, and that by presenting the ideas as a list of strategies I could show clearly how the methodology works and provide a useful summary.

Years later, I am still using the same approach, and I have found that as well as the professionals, there are many amateurs who are keen to find out how markets work and how to improve their investment performance. These are the secrets that they want to discover.

Structure of the book

In this book I reveal those secrets and the thrills and pains I experienced in finding them. Many of these ideas and philosophies are now being adopted by successful hedge funds. They are presented as 100 different Strategies spread evenly over ten chapters.

Chapter 1 – Markets

My first trading experience resulted in a big loss. I was lucky! I quickly learnt how tough it can be. The most common mistake is to assume that investment success is easy. This is encouraged by so-called 'expert' views appearing in the media which imply that market prices are somehow flawed and that there are plenty of opportunities.

The irony is that in thinking it's too easy, investors make it more difficult! It leads them away from the truth. The starting point must be that market prices are normally about right, and that any opportunities can only be found by identifying their cause and understanding how they work. We need to be careful – experts are vastly overrated. Most professionals in the markets are not actually outguessing the price, but are making money from clients, transactions and commissions.

The markets are increasingly challenging. Many opportunities that investors pursued years ago have simply disappeared. Speculation increasingly requires that the fundamentals are fully supportive. Even governments find it hard to push prices to the wrong levels.

Fortunately I have found one shortcut in the investment world which works very well: the approach in these Strategies can be used for many different markets. I have used the same methods successfully over twenty years with currencies, bonds, property, stocks and private companies. It has enabled me to pursue investment opportunities wherever they may be found.

Chapter 2 – Comparative Advantages

An investor needs to spot genuine opportunities in order to make good consistent returns. A few market professionals can rely on the advantages of superior information, high quality analysis or client orders to help them predict future price moves, but for various reasons these advantages are dwindling, and anyway the ordinary investor needs something more accessible. Fortunately there are opportunities offered by market behaviour which are long lasting and can be spotted without enormous research or inside information:

- There remain patterns and anomalies in the markets.
- Markets are slow to react to big picture changes.
- Small companies offer more opportunities.
- Markets go further than generally expected.
- Markets move in underlying trends.
- A view on the fundamentals can be combined with price movements to manage trading positions.

When these are pursued with sensible risk management the results can be stunning.

Chapter 3 – Risk

Over a period of time, even the best investors will inevitably suffer losses. Unfortunately even good ideas can lose money just as bad ideas can sometimes make money. There is inevitably a high degree of chance or luck involved. The most important thing is to manage the risks and to 'stay in the game'. Investors need to think about how far a price can move in the wrong direction. They also need to diversify, be able to cut losing positions and withstand the stress involved.

Chapter 4 – Patterns and Anomalies

I have spent my professional life looking for patterns and anomalies. There are many in the markets which are useful to understand. Shares, bonds, currencies and property all offer unique challenges and opportunities.

A good idea can often point to more than one type of investment. One example is that a strong economy is bullish for both stocks and property, but property may be the easier play because it has smoother cycles.

Another pattern in the markets is that crisis situations almost always provide opportunities to those investors who can remain calm and who have kept some powder dry.

Chapter 5 – Big Ideas

Big ideas can make big money. There is a host of examples: the big falls in inflation, technological innovation, emerging economies and China's appetite for raw materials are just a few. The big ideas cause big but slow changes in many markets. Seldom are these expected by economists and analysts who often struggle to see the wood for the trees.

Investors should look for these big ideas and ignore anything which is too obscure. With those small things it is normally too difficult to out-analyse the analysts.

For investors in mainstream markets, the big idea they are pursuing is often the state of the economy. It's too hard, for example, to make money on the broad stock market when the economy is going into a recession, so at that time bonds are a better bet. A useful way for those investors to keep an eye on the economy is by a simple checklist of the positives and negatives.

Chapter 6 – Small Companies

I am convinced that small companies offer more opportunities than larger companies. There is a greater chance that they are mis-priced in the market because there is a big variation in their quality, they are often involved with new products and they are not as widely followed by analysts and investors.

For a small company, the competence of the management is the most important feature. Other things investors need to look at are, of course, the company's products and markets and its ability to handle growth.

Chapter 7 – Price Behaviour

Time and time again I have watched market prices go a long way and surprise just about everybody involved. In recent years, there have been moves, like the rise and fall in the NASDAQ, the rise in the oil price, the rise in house prices and the weakness of the US dollar. These market moves are opportunities, because in each case the market takes its time to react to big ideas and big changes. All the way along, people are sceptical and they don't expect the price move to continue, so investors need to expect the unexpected. They shouldn't cut winning positions too early, and they should accept that the old price levels are history.

Chapter 8 – The Understanding and Use of Trends in Prices

I am able to show that trends have operated across nearly all markets for a long, long time. These price trends are a gift! A market that has moved higher is more likely to continue moving higher than to suddenly reverse. The equivalent applies for a falling market. Although trends are well known in the markets, their implications are ignored (even denied!) by mainstream thinking. For example, despite the common belief, markets tend to under-react, not overreact. Trends can be used to make money; for years I have experienced a lot of success using simple systems which use nothing but trends, and trends can help decide the best way to time investments.

There are solid reasons why trends exist and will persist in the future. Market information spreads gradually, and the reaction is delayed by inertia and scepticism. Rising prices can actually lead to more, rather than less, buying in the market. Economic cycles also help prices move in trends.

Chapter 9 – Market Timing

Even the best investment ideas can come unstuck due to bad decisions on when to buy and sell. The best technique for entering the market is to wait for a price trend to verify a bullish or bearish view. So it is not a good idea – unless there is market panic – to buy into falling markets. Being a contrarian means fighting against trends and not acknowledging that markets can go further than expected. It may work occasionally, but it is against the odds. Similarly, add to winning trades, not losing trades, and don't be scared if you are investing alongside the consensus view. For a price to go a long way it will require consensus agreement at some point.

The decision to exit should only be made when the reasons for the investment are no longer sound, or when the price trend has reversed. Sticking with winning trades for as long as possible is the only way to make big wins.

Chapter 10 – Avoiding Temptation

I believe that really good investors can avoid temptation. They have the discipline to know when there are no genuine opportunities and not to take excessive risks. In these situations, it may be useful to keep an eye on a variety of markets and to see if any price trends develop. These may signal when something is happening which is worth investigating.

Be careful in these quiet times, because even simple wealth preservation is not straight forward due to taxes and inflation. Sophisticated retail products may appear good on the surface but require close scrutiny. With a passive portfolio, management and brokerage fees should be kept to a minimum.

A brief biography

By Janine Perrett

I first met Richard in 2000 through mutual friends. He had just helped turn a rundown Georgian mansion in London into a successful private members' club, and he was being lauded in the business pages for his support of emerging technology companies.

He was, in short, an ideal candidate for a story on my Business Sunday programme on the national Nine Network in Australia, particularly as, despite his success, he was not widely known in his homeland.

After the programme aired in May 2001, we were inundated with hundreds of letters and emails, many hailing his success, many more emotionally moved and inspired by his personal triumph over the odds.

Here is his story.

The country town of Kyabram lies 200 kilometres north-west of Melbourne in the southern Australian state of Victoria. In 1960 it had fewer than 5,000 residents but it boasted the newly opened Kyabram District Memorial Community Hospital, and it was here, on November 9th that Richard Buckland Smith was born.

His middle name was a nod to his ancestors who can trace their roots back five generations to the infamous Rum Corps rebellion. Such long links are important in such a young country where being a sixth generation Australian is something to be proud of. In fact the name was probably the only thing the troubled family had to be proud of at that moment in their history.

His father, Richard Geddes Smith, was probably just passing through Kyabram at the time of the birth, as his occupation is variously described as shearer, opal miner and seasonal labourer. His mother, the former Millicent Duggan, had already borne much, including seven other children; Richard was only the second boy. Before he was born, a baby sister had died after drinking bad water from a river close to where the family had camped.

In his brief time with his natural family Richard never knew what it was like to have a proper home, or even live in a normal house. They travelled the countryside in an old truck with all the children in the back, open to the elements. Rodney Smith, who was eight when his brother Richard was born, recalls when the weather was bad they would all sing "rain rain go away, let us live in a house one day". A tent was carried in the truck to shelter them all when they next made camp.

Rodney does not dwell on the unpleasant aspects of their childhood except to concede he suffered a fractured skull once courtesy of his alcoholic father. There's no doubt it was a violent childhood as Richard reluctantly recalls his very first memory was one of "fear".

When Richard was barely two years old, all the children were taken into care by the State. The fact that so many children were taken from their parents indicates how appalling, even then, the authorities regarded their situation. Being the 1960s, the unenlightened Australian social welfare system made no attempt to keep the children together. They were all split up, never to be reunited as a family.

Probably because he was still only a baby, Richard did not have to spend too long in the home as he was soon taken into foster care by Marjorie and Keith Farleigh from Peakhurst in Sydney's south-western suburbs.

Marjorie's first impression of her new son was that "he was a lovely little boy", but even though she thought he looked healthy, he soon came down with a terrible bout of measles. During the illness one of his eyes 'turned' and he was forced to wear a patch. Richard was confined to a darkened room with daily visits from the doctor. It would take two operations to correct the problem and by then he was five and already at school.

The Farleighs were under the impression they were only minding Richard for a few months until his parents wanted him returned. In fact Marjorie kept his bag and all his clothes packed and ready for when they sent him back. However she decided this delicate little boy needed her, so the next time the welfare officer visited, she informed him "Richard will be staying".

Apart from one strained reunion when he was four, Richard had no contact with his natural family while growing up. While the Smiths had three other children, some of whom they simply gave away, as well as the seven who were fostered out at the same time as Richard, it was not until he was an adult that he made contact with his other siblings.

His mother died in the 1990s and he lost track of his father – in fact the last time he recalls seeing him was a chance meeting at a Sydney railway station where his itinerant father was sitting on a bench with his harmonica and swag.

While it's clear Richard was lucky in finding a stable home with a loving foster mother and two caring foster brothers, Peter and Ian, his relationship with his foster father was never close.

Richard's first kindergarten teachers placed him in the lowest class as they misinterpreted his chronic shyness and reluctance to speak as a sign of being backward. A turning point came in Year 5 at Peakhurst Primary school when he was about eight years old and was lucky enough to get into the class of a teacher called Jan Walker. She is still at Peakhurst, a principal these days, and recalls her first impressions of Richard as being small for his age and very shy, but even then she recognised his aptitude.

She remembers:

"He was a ghost in class and his self-esteem was not great. He was not doing well in English, but he was far ahead in mathematics and I told him - 'you have a lot of potential. You haven't reached it yet and you won't do it for a long time, but you're going to do well'."

It was after he entered Narwee Boys High that another important turning point came for the introverted youngster. At the age of 12 his brother Peter taught him to play chess. It was to change his life.

"I was pretty unhappy the whole time I was at high school, but chess made me feel a bit better." Richard says, "Suddenly I really started not to believe the negative things I felt about myself".

For Richard, the game that started out as hobby soon became a passion and he quickly rose to the rank of Junior State Champion. A whole new life opened up as he travelled the country attending chess tournaments, making new friends and finding a previously unknown confidence in his ability. Years later he would represent Bermuda and Monaco in the Chess Olympics.

After high school Richard decided to study economics at the University of New South Wales, and by topping an exam he won a generous scholarship from the Australian central bank. He graduated with first class honours in economics and econometrics but decided against doing a PhD, and chose instead to accept a job offer from the leading Australian investment bank of the time, Bankers Trust Australia.

Still shy and lacking confidence, the 23 year old began working in the derivatives business for the then CEO who reportedly told colleagues he doubted the youngster would ever succeed and that "if he makes a buck for the bank, I'll walk backwards to Bourke". That's nearly 800 kilometres from Sydney.

Richard ended up becoming the bank's biggest single money earner.

In his 1999 book, *One of a Kind: The Story of Bankers Trust Australia 1969-1999*, writer Gideon Haigh described Richard as "one of the most fascinating characters" to pass through the investment bank:

"As he began taking more views and more risks, Farleigh's earnings and reputation grew. He evolved some first principles of trading. Markets tended to overreact in the short term and under-react in the long term. Investors tended to work off price rather than fundamentals.

He was militantly against chance. He was also out of sympathy with other trading schools reliant on data mining and regression analysis. His modus operandi was forward-looking - if a, then b, suggesting c - and his mentality that of a purist:

'I hated it if you put a position on and it just happened to work, because I felt that left you with nothing for next time. I didn't like charts, either. That was hocus-pocus. I was a fundamental trader. That's much harder than being a technical trader.' "

In the book, Richard's former boss, Bruce Hogan, recalls:

"Richard always had a very clear view of how the market would unfold. And, when it didn't go according to expectations, his disciplines getting out were intense. Even when Richard made losses, I was always impressed with the rigour of his post-mortems. Was it a bad decision? Or was it actually still a good risk-return decision where something of a lower probability happened?"

By 1993 Richard was in his early 30s and earning a seven figure sum as the star trader, when he was headhunted for a powerful and secretive international hedge fund based in Bermuda. On this idyllic island tax haven he was able to refine the crucial trading style which he had been developing at Bankers. He described his three years here as "trader's heaven".

He did well enough to retire to Monaco at only 34 with his then wife Sharon and baby son Thomas. From this tiny tax haven filled with wealthy individuals from around the globe, he began to look for other opportunities to make money outside the strict constraints of the trading floor. So he turned his hand from currencies and interest rates to UK tech stocks and in the following years he backed over 50 early stage companies.

By the time the 'tech wreck' began in 2000, Farleigh had been investing in technology for five years. While he was hit by inevitable and difficult losses, his earlier profits provided him with a crucial buffer, and with the recovery of the market, some of his companies now read like a who's who of new market listings in UK technology.

While he was pursuing this investment activity, another, totally different opportunity presented itself in the form of Home House. This architectural masterpiece, which had once housed the French Embassy during the Revolution, was on a list of the world's 100 endangered buildings. The idea was to restore the building and to make a fantastic private members' club.

"It would be nice to be an Australian saving one of the Pommys' endangered buildings", he said with a touch of the larrikin.

And it worked. The club soon became the most sought after venue in London, with a celebrity-filled membership list including Madonna and a host of numerous high profile functions including a big 'Brit Awards' after-party. Even though Richard and his partners sold out of the club in 2004 he still maintains strong ties and visits frequently.

He continues as an active investor in early stage technology companies.

Richard now has another two children, Jasmine and Lucas, with his partner Camilla, and they divide their time between Monaco and London.

Janine Perrett

Sydney, May 2005

On father's shoulders - before the children were taken into care by the authorities

A day in the life

In the first Gulf War, US forces overwhelmingly attacked Iraqi forces in Kuwait. It was an awesome display of military power, and almost the whole world was surprised and amazed at how powerful the US military had become. They had moved to a new level: missiles with cameras attached that could be steered through the front doors of buildings, and strange looking black planes called 'stealth bombers' that were invisible to radar. Iraq's feeble response looked hollow following Saddam Hussein's earlier "mother of all battles" threats, but if he could have mustered enough anti-American sentiment in other Arab nations, he may have pulled an armed rabbit out of the hat.

Financial markets around the globe were preoccupied with the battle. The oil market was naturally the most affected; the spot price per barrel was driven from the high teens to over 40 dollars, as traders contemplated a huge disruption in supply. The stock market worried about the recession that would result if the oil price stayed so high for too long. Interest rates were pushed sharply higher by the potential inflationary effect of the rising oil price.

Traders in the markets all scrambled to learn as much as they could about oil and the Middle East as quickly as possible. It was a change from the boring old employment numbers and inflation figures which everyone normally had to scrutinise. If Saddam set alight oil wells, as he threatened, would they really burn for a hundred years, or could they be extinguished by having big domes put over the top? And what would happen if he spilled a massive load of oil into the sea and set it on fire? Anyone who might know the answers suddenly got their fifteen minutes of fame. Oil experts were brought into the trading rooms and treated like celebrities as their information was needed to make a rational view of any of the markets.

From a trading room in Sydney, my perspective was just as confused as anyone else's. Even though my job was to take risks with money, there was no way I had any competitive edge to allow me to think the markets had got something wrong. For the previous year or so I had been betting strongly on falls in interest rates. I believed that the economy would be weaker than generally expected and that inflation would be driven lower. For me this war was an interruption to a slow economic trend. War was too risky for a bet and I had cashed in my chips – I was out of the market.

Although I didn't want to bet, I could still watch. Investors were looking for safe places to put their money: the gold price and the American dollar had risen. For gold a rally was normal – during a world crisis gold is the hero. It's all about probabilities. Even if the world's not about to end, there is a slightly greater chance of chaos. Paper money relies on people's confidence in a government, whereas gold has intrinsic value. In post-war Germany, people needed a sack full of money to buy bread. If they had bought gold earlier they could have maintained their wealth. So the market's extremely sensitive barometer to chaos was rocked by the Gulf War, and the gold price had been pushed significantly higher. Another reason gold rallied was the inflationary threat of the higher oil price, because inflation is bad for paper money but good for commodities.

The rally in the dollar also made sense. During a crisis it makes sense to have your money in the hands of a superpower, especially when you've seen the effectiveness of their military on CNN.

When Iraq started lobbing missiles into Israel, the war reached a critical stage. Saddam's thinking was simple: if Israel could be provoked into retaliating, other Arab nations would see a broadening of the issues and perhaps come to Iraq's defence.

Time passed. The dollar climbed even higher. I think gold was actually starting to struggle to hold its gains, and I remember thinking: "If gold can't go higher on this news, when on earth will it? Maybe it's time for investors to sell?" However the only bet I took was against the dollar. I reasoned that Israel would listen to the US, who would instruct them not to retaliate under any circumstances. Given that the allied forces were clearly superior, if there was no broadening of the conflict, the markets would soon calm down. So I sold dollars for marks and waited.

Fortunately for the world (and for me), Israel stayed passive and I was then able to close my position for a profit as the dollar later declined.

It can be profitable and exhilarating — but let's start at the beginning

With the story above I have tried to reveal some of the thoughts that ran through my mind while I was trading. Investment can be nerve-racking and exciting. Even when there is confusion everywhere, it is possible to find ways to succeed by using logic and by understanding how markets work.

These are the things I love to discuss and analyse. However, in this book I need to start at the beginning. The first two or three chapters are essentially warnings and background ideas. Please be patient. Only after covering that material can we get into the fun part of how I believe you can make money from trading and investment.

With Peter and Marjorie Farleigh

1 | Markets

1.0 The different markets have many useful similarities

As a youngster my first ambition was to be a bushranger just like Ned Kelly. This nineteenth century outlaw was Australia's own Robin Hood, except that he fought against police injustice wearing his bullet-proof helmet and vest made from steel. Eventually caught and sentenced to hang, his last words were "such is life".

My ambitions improved slightly as I grew older, and in my teens I thought of being a religious minister, or of trying my luck as a professional chess player. These things faded, however, and as I finished high school in Sydney in the late 1970s, my plan was to be an economist. The little bit of economics that I had learnt had whetted my appetite. Economics is often criticised as the 'dismal science', and there is a joke at its expense which states that you could line up all the economists in the world and still not reach a conclusion. But I had good teachers, and one of them in particular, Peter Rolfe, showed me that economics achieved a hell of a lot by starting with some quite acceptable assumptions about human behaviour. From there, it is able to do a reasonable job with the daunting task of predicting the actions of millions of people when wages, prices, interest rates, taxes and other financial factors change. Peter is a fun and sporty person, so he was quite an evangelist for the subject.

A few years later, I had finished my degree and found myself working in the Research Department of the Reserve Bank of Australia, which is Australia's central bank. From there, however, I made a quick career change and entered the hyper-competitive world of investment banking. I had been told that the money was good, but that you had to be able to handle the stress. I remember thinking "hmm, I'll try to make some money, and I'll worry about the stress later".

My career since then has been unusual because, as a trader and investor, I have been involved with many different types of markets. Since the early 1980s I have been a derivatives trader, a bond trader, a currency trader, a business angel and a stock investor. I have worked for an investment bank, a private hedge fund and for myself, managing my own funds. I have been very lucky because I have enjoyed all of it immensely, and I have produced good returns for others and myself along the way.

The most striking and satisfying thing that I have learnt from this experience is that the different markets have many similarities. This is contrary to what many people expect. I believe that in all markets:

- Any genuine opportunity needs to be based on a sound observation.
- Big ideas offer big opportunities.
- Prices take time to absorb information.
- Prices go further than generally expected.
- Prices move in trends.
- Crisis situations and panic buying or selling occur from time to time.
- Investing requires a sensible approach to risk management.
- Analysis requires recognition of both the bullish and the bearish arguments. A checklist is very useful.
- 'Experts' are often wrong, and the media oversell how easy it is to make money.

Because of these similarities, the various investing and trading opportunities offer the same types of challenges and opportunities, and they can be approached in much the same manner. I have even found that, for example, investing in an unlisted biotech company involves some similar skills to trading euros versus the dollar.

The ability for an investor to change focus can be very useful as investment opportunities shift from one market to another. In the late 80s and early 90s there were fantastic investments offered by the big falls in interest rates in the western economies. For nearly a decade after that opportunity waned, it was the stock market which had a brilliant run. More recently, commodities have been surging.

Investors and traders who only look at one type of market can be trapped without these big opportunities. They are trying to grow flowers in the desert. Sometimes, it can be useful to move elsewhere.

Consequently the 100 Strategies are applicable to a very broad range of investments. The idea is to find the right ideas and not waste time and money trying to eke out a return from barren areas.

Trading and investment are increasingly similar

It is probably best to clarify at this early stage that I believe trading and investment are increasingly similar. Traditionally, there is a distinct difference between the two. Investment is putting wealth into different markets with a long term view. Adjustments to the portfolio are made infrequently and at a slow pace. Trading, on the other hand, is holding positions for shorter periods of time, looking to make a faster profit, and then exiting. Investment tends to be buy and hold, whereas trading tends to be based on temporary reasons with an exit when those temporary reasons have dissipated.

However, successful investment increasingly recognises that the buy and hold strategy may not work. It may require a more timely response to what's happening in the markets, since they can move a long way in a fairly short period of time.

Equally, as we will see, many short term trading opportunities in the markets no longer exist, and now the best opportunities may have a time horizon that extends into months and even years.

So, in these Strategies, I will not try to distinguish between trading and investing, and I will use the terms interchangeably.

Fundamentals

I will also use the term market 'fundamentals'. These are all the factors affecting a market. Anything that influences, or potentially influences, demand and supply is a fundamental, whether it's social, economic, political or the natural environment.

1.1 Fear the market

My first ever trading experience was a disaster. In 1984, fresh out of university, I started trading futures in my spare time. Futures can be very risky because of the leverage – whereby a small deposit can give you a large exposure to price moves.

I can't remember why I was ever tempted into trading, but I do remember the result: over a few months I lost four thousand dollars. It was a lot of money to me, which I couldn't really afford since, as a trainee, I was earning less than twenty thousand a year.

My mistakes

I had no experience and I did all the wrong things:

- I started with positions which were way too big.
- I stopped and started a new strategy every few days.
- I had no long term view.
- I didn't really understand what was driving the market.
- I grabbed profits as soon as I could and stayed with losing positions.
- I listened to the views of other people who probably had no idea either, including brokers and people with fancy charts.

The result was to scare the life out of me. I had thought you could make money by trading, but I became convinced that it was impossible. I squared all of my positions and decided never to trade again.

Although it did not take long for me to break that vow, I have never forgotten that first unpleasant experience. Even now, when I make investments, I have a fear of the markets, and perhaps an underlying scepticism of my ability to outwit them. However, I am convinced that over the years, the fear I first experienced at that time has saved me a lot of money, and allowed me to stay in the business of trading.

I want you to have that same level of respect. I want to convince you that the market can be a horrible place where your money can just disappear very quickly. You're throwing dice, tossing coins, whatever. There are no certainties and you don't know what you're up against.

"A hard way to make an easy living"

Cleanse yourself of any idea that it's easy. You're in for a difficult time. Like me, most traders and investors have had to learn this the hard way, at one time or another, by losing money and agonising over bad positions. By giving you this warning I'm trying to save you from that nightmare.

The market is much more difficult than you think. It acts like a huge super-computer as it effectively absorbs an unbelievable amount of information — more than any human being could fathom.

When you buy or sell in the market you are hoping that the current market price is wrong, that the super-computer is wrong. Now stop for a moment and think how incredible that would be. If you believe that the dollar will fall, what you actually believe is that the current price is flawed, even though it is the result of a huge amount of people dealing in a huge amount of money.

For that reason, when I am asked for my view on a currency or another market, I'm very reluctant to disagree with the price as it stands. I personally give the markets that level of respect — and I've been battling them with some success for a long time. Yet many people who lack any experience will happily put forward their view with an astonishing degree of unfounded confidence.

Don't forget that these days there is intense analysis by funds and banks and that they still regularly get it wrong — often spectacularly wrong. So start with a degree of caution. Be like a lion tamer. The lion can be tamed, but only by maintaining a healthy fear of the lion.

1.2 Markets are more efficient than generally acknowledged

I often think of the market as an opponent, a living being to outwit and defeat. To 'beat the market' we need to look for weaknesses in our opponent's armoury. The problem is that our opponent is nearly

> I often think of the market as an opponent, a living being to outwit and defeat.

perfect. It is very 'efficient' at setting prices that offer no opportunities. If we buy and sell on just whims, or on unfounded ideas, we cannot win the battle.

Efficiency in markets is a concept stemming from economics. Quite simply, an efficient market is unbeatable. It sets a price whereby you may as well toss a coin to decide whether to buy or sell. At any time, the price completely reflects all relevant information. There is no point taking the view that because of factor X, a market is undervalued; factor X is already known and factored into the current price.

No opportunities in an efficient market

One consequence of an efficient market is that prices move in a random manner. All current information is already reflected in the current price, which means that the price can only move in response to new (and thereby, as yet, unknowable) news. Therefore there is no trend, and no one can predict what the price is going to do next.

Microsoft shares could be a good example of market efficiency. As I write, their price in New York is $24.91. This is the price that reflects all the known information about Microsoft. As ongoing information emerges about the company, it is disseminated quickly, traders buy and sell on the basis of that information, and the price moves accordingly. Your guess is as good as anyone's about where the price will go from here.

An efficient market offers us no opportunities. It is an opponent without weaknesses.

Fortunately, markets are not always efficient

Luckily for us, however, the markets are not always efficient. The most likely reasons that a market fails to operate efficiently are that:

- All the relevant information is not equally available to all buyers and sellers. An example would be a bargain in the property market which exists because too few buyers are aware of the opportunity.
- The buyers and sellers all have the relevant information but do not sufficiently understand the implications of that information. Here an example would be when people continue to pay high prices for property even when they know that the economy is going into recession.

Occasionally, it is suggested that some illiquid markets – where there are not many buyers and sellers – are inefficient because they can be unfairly dominated by a few players. However I will argue later that those players usually lose out.

It is possible that markets are inefficient when they are deliberately fed misleading information, as happened with Enron and Worldcom, but hopefully that type of malpractice is on the decline.

With these Strategies, I will try to identify, in a very structured and disciplined manner, where it is that I believe the market does not operate efficiently. This is where we will find opportunities to beat the market.

Unfortunately, most people do not approach trading and investing in that way. Rather, they start with an assumption that the markets are inefficient and that there are obvious buy or sell opportunities. They have vague, untested beliefs, and make comments like 'the consensus is always wrong', or 'the market always overshoots'. Both of which we will see are completely untrue.

1.3 Market opportunities are disappearing

When I entered the world of finance in the mid 1980s I was fortunate enough to join the right investment bank: Bankers Trust Australia. With a reputation as the highest paying employer in Australia, it was *the* place to work. The people were very creative and motivated, and it operated as a genuine meritocracy with little bureaucracy or politics. At one stage, in terms of percentage return on capital, it was rated as one of the most profitable banks in the world.

I was put to work in the trading room, which I found amazing. I was a bee in a beehive – all around me there was activity. There were about a hundred of us in the room, with lots of screens and telephones and paper everywhere. There were all types of people, and most of them were very engaging and friendly. Everywhere, the mood was generally upbeat and there was a lot of joking around.

The room was divided into a number of different departments: foreign exchange, bonds, money market, options, and the area I joined, cross-markets. With a mix of clever people and abundant market opportunities, all of the departments were humming along making money.

It was a time when the winds of change were howling through the markets. By aiding their design, personal computers were allowing financial products to become far more sophisticated - the abacus and slide rule could be thrown in the bin! Improved communications such as mobile phones were making it easier to keep track of what was going on around the world.

On top of this, governments were encouraging greater competition in the financial sector. The lazy old-fashioned banker, who enjoyed boozy lunches and golf days, no longer found life so easy. Suddenly there was pressure to offer competitive prices and to be more innovative.

The search for market inconsistencies

In cross-markets, one of our roles was to look for market inconsistencies, and to take advantage of them using the bank's own funds. We were also responsible for the pricing of swaps, (sophisticated products that can protect businesses from volatility in currencies, interest rates and other markets).

Both of these activities were slightly complicated, but they were relatively low risk because we would simultaneously buy in one type of market and sell in another, leaving us with only a small exposure to market moves. After getting a grip on the mathematics involved, we usually had some time to plan our strategies, and to allow our positions to bear fruit. This type of thing suited me. I would never have made the grade if my job was to juggle phones like the book makers, or shout at the top of my voice like the floor traders. I liked having the chance to think, and to be able to watch things unfold over time.

Due to the relatively low risk, we were able to really go for it – our trades involved very large sums of money. So, here I was in my early twenties, with a few grand in the bank, a cheap suit and no real experience, and I was on the phone doing deals worth tens and hundreds of millions. I was so happy to feel that important. I knew I'd been given a big chance, and I didn't want to mess it up. I had to be careful and check the calculations carefully before I did anything. Even a slip of the tongue could be dangerous, because saying 'buy' instead of 'sell' could obviously cost a lot of money. Once I fretted for an entire weekend thinking I had made just that mistake. On the Monday, I found that I hadn't. The relief was like waking from a bad dream.

I stayed in this role for three or four years, and during that time we enjoyed a lot of success despite the low risks. It was great, there were no major problems and I became accustomed to dealing in large amounts of other people's money. It was lucrative too. I had nervously taken a pay cut when I joined Bankers Trust, but my salary took off like a rocket and continued to rise while I was at the Bank. Starting at twenty thousand dollars at the age of twenty four, it more or less doubled every year: to fifty, one hundred, two hundred and fifty, five hundred, and then to one million and beyond by the age of thirty. That was big money, especially fifteen years ago. My friends couldn't believe it, and I couldn't believe it would go on. So, like a squirrel, I saved just about all of it.

Not so easy now

As I look back on that era, it's clear that a lot of the ways that our trading room made money have simply disappeared. The markets have become relentlessly more sophisticated as the changes that started in the early 80s have continued. Nowadays, everyone is extremely well qualified, there are computer programs everywhere and there are instant communications. The market has evolved, like bacteria against antibiotics, to beat out opportunities. This has happened as people have spotted opportunities and exploited them till they no longer exist.

So over the years, as my career progressed, I have looked for high quality opportunities which are somehow resilient. I will present these in later chapters and explain why I believe they have persisted while others have been eliminated.

1.4 The markets can overwhelm government intervention

In September 1985 the world's biggest governments met at the Plaza Hotel in New York and reached an agreement: the US dollar was over-valued and needed to fall.

The effect was stunning. With the market aware of the new "official" preference for a weaker dollar, and some ten billion worth of dollars sold into the market by the governments as a show of force, the dollar dropped dramatically. In the following two years or so, it halved in value versus the other major currencies. An astonishing success for government policy.

However, this success was more of an exception than a rule. In fact, markets are normally too big to be bullied.

Countries of all sizes have often been tempted to try to dictate the value of their currency by intervening in the markets. Sometimes they want to lower a strong currency, but more often they want to prop up a weak currency. In some cases a falling exchange rate can be seen as an embarrassing assessment of political integrity and economic performance.

So governments enter the market with one thing in mind: to move the price. They buy or sell aggressively, and may add to the drama with a big announcement about government policy and commitment. The effect is immediate. Like a shark at a beach they cause widespread panic. Speculators and dealing rooms all over the world scramble to adjust their positions, and the media give the news top priority.

It was in the middle of one such episode a few years ago, when I had the idea to investigate the longer term effect of government intervention. The government was intervening aggressively in the Australian dollar market and there was a flurry of activity around me in the dealing room. Looking at the prices flashing on the screen, I wondered if the market reaction was very long lasting. Sure enough, my subsequent research showed that while falling currencies typically bounce after government action, in less than a month or so, they resume on their downward path and continue to weaken towards fresh lows.

So by spotting this pattern I had found a new, profitable strategy. Whenever the market had this kind of knee-jerk reaction to government intervention, I would bet against it, on the assumption that the bounce was only temporary. I was effectively backing market fundamentals versus the government.

The fact that even governments, with all their muscle, cannot reverse the market has always impressed me. It shows the depth and efficiency of the financial markets.

Keep that in mind when you think that the market price is wrong.

1.5 The market is strengthened by speculation

Over the years I have heard a great deal of criticism about speculators. It often pops up when markets or currencies are having a dramatic fall. Funny, speculation doesn't seem to bother so many people when it's pushing prices higher. Should speculators be ashamed? No, the fact is that the market needs them.

Speculators add important liquidity. I often invest in small stocks, which would not have much daily turnover if it were not for speculators. The longer term holders of these stocks do not buy or sell very often, so when I need to find a buyer or a seller, it is a great benefit to have speculators as they are much more active.

Speculators also play an important role in absorbing risk that others don't want. Wheat farmers, for example, may sell their crop well before harvest at a fixed price for a future delivery date. That way, they can remove the risk that there is a bumper season and an oversupply that forces prices lower. The buyers may be speculators who are happy to take on that risk – without the speculators, the farmers may have no one to sell to.

You often hear criticism of speculation based on the flawed argument that it pushes prices to unrealistic levels. The thing is though, speculators are usually punished when they do this, because if they are wrong about real values, they are usually the big losers. The tech boom and bust, where perhaps it was speculators who drove prices to very high levels, is a great example. Most of them paid very heavily when market prices crashed to a fraction of the higher levels. Though what a great opportunity it was for the more savvy investors to sell near the highs.

So, speculation is usually only successful when it is in line with the fundamentals, and when it is pushing prices to a level that more closely reflects fair value.

George Soros and Black Wednesday

A great example of this is George Soros. He has been criticised because his massive selling probably caused the devaluation of the British Pound in 1992. In fact the resulting weaker currency and lower interest rates saved the UK economy, because they were more appropriate for the conditions at the time. The date (16th September 1992) is known as 'Black Wednesday' because the currency was pushed out of the European Exchange Rate Mechanism (ERM), but in my view it should be renamed 'White Wednesday'. That day is one reason that the UK has only five per cent unemployment, while Europe, which stuck with cripplingly high interest rates for way too long, has about ten per cent. The feeling was that Soros was a greedy speculator who made a billion pounds in profit, but in fact it has proved to be a very cheap price for the British, because the lower pound - and the resulting lower interest rates – allowed for a big improvement in the economy. If the man in the street knew how things worked, Soros would be seen as a hero, not a villain!

For this reason, many commentators are naïve when they criticise these price shocks and the speculators involved. It can be better to have wild swings in currencies and other prices than lots of people losing their livelihoods.

It was a similar case in the late 1990s, when Malaysian Prime Minister Mahathir attacked currency speculators because they were pushing down the value of his currency. Again, speculation wouldn't have worked unless there was a solid reason behind it. A few years later, the consensus is that the currency was too high for the economic conditions at the time.

The speculator is often just the messenger.

1.6 Respect the market not the experts

The power of the financial markets should be daunting, but many people are not deterred.

I have friends in Monaco who are amateur currency traders. They don't have the same experience, resources, or the skill, of a George Soros. Nor do they follow the disciplined approach to trading that is recommended in this book. It's completely crazy that they think they can win. Why do people underestimate the difficulty of making money in the financial markets? I believe there are two main reasons.

The first, which I will discuss here, is the experts in the media. The second is the widely held belief that many professionals are regularly able to beat the market. This I will discuss in the following Strategy. I won't dwell on a possible third reason, which is that some people like to trade the market because they are gamblers. That usually ends with disastrous results.

'Experts'?

The experts in the media promote the idea that markets are easier than they really are. A guy on TV or in the newspaper says that the price is going to do this and do that, and it sounds easy. The market can be beaten.

If the media put out a continual broadcast that the market has processed all the information and that the price is right, people would get the message. But they rarely say that. The message is that the behaviour of the market can be forecasted. It's a persistent and seductive message, and people think 'ah, I can have a go at that, I can make money out of that'. You can't blame the average person for following what they read in the newspaper and what they're being told on TV. However, many so-called experts are just commentators or analysts who often don't have any track record and who often, to my ear, don't even make much sense. Follow my advice below and listen critically, rather than just accept what you're hearing or reading. You may be surprised to find that they're not really experts.

Not that I blame the media for their financial guesswork. It can be very entertaining. But like a lot of gossip, the fact that it's entertaining and interesting doesn't necessarily mean that it's the truth.

1.7 Most professionals are not outguessing the market

You may heed my early warnings that the markets are difficult and that the media underplays the difficulties, but you may also wonder about all the money made by the people working on Wall Street or in the City of London. Surely they know something about markets?

Let me put you straight on this. The truth is that very few are successfully backing their views on markets. Most of them wouldn't have a clue what the market was going to do. They make money in other ways, such as commission and management fees.

It's not that people working in finance don't know anything – they are usually very good, very smart people. I respect a lot of them and many are my friends – but the fact is they're making money out of sales, client relationships and by doing transactions, i.e. facilitating the whole process. They're not actually making money out of successfully predicting what's going to go up and down. They are, therefore, not a reason for you to take up punting cotton futures in your spare time.

Equally, don't be too impressed with your stockbroker just because they sound confident and know a lot of stories and figures. More information does not necessarily make the market more predictable. The extra information is probably useless as the price has already adjusted for it - it has been 'priced in'. It's about as useful as playing roulette and knowing whether the roulette wheel was made in Taiwan or Korea. The critical test is: does the broker make a living out of picking stocks? Probably not. He or she is sitting in their seat because they're getting the fees you pay them to buy and sell on your behalf. It's very easy for someone to have a view when it's with someone else's money.

1.8 Listen and read very critically

If you are trading or investing, the media probably plays a large role in forming your views, but it always surprises me how often they present faulty logic. So it is vital to learn to be critical of what you read and hear.

Try to spot mistakes such as those in the following real examples.

"Experts say the market is overvalued."

This is a subject I have already touched on. 'Experts' is the most overused word in finance. I see it all the time and wonder who these experts are! The only expert who interests me is someone with a proven track record of predicting the market. As we have seen, most professionals are not capable of outguessing the market, and those that do are not normally very interested in telling the media about their thoughts.

What's more, you can normally find an expert somewhere to support any view at all. Perhaps the journalist has a heavy workload and just rang a friend at a bank, arranged to meet for a drink, asked about the market, and relayed this as 'experts say the market is overvalued'.

"The money market predicts rates will rise from 3.5% today to 5% by late next year...The good news is that such predictions are probably wrong... Many analysts see rates reaching no higher than 4.5% in 18 months."

These 'analysts' are a bit like the experts. I would have more faith in the market's view. Those analysts are free to put their money where their mouth is and bet against the market if they want, but I've rarely met any with enough skill or conviction.

"With the euro at $1.25 a sustainable range is $1.22 to $1.28. Upside risks predominate though a short term drop to $1.15 is not out of the question."

This is a bet each way. The easiest forecast to make is something like: if the price doesn't rise, it will fall, or perhaps even stay the same. It's useless.

"The pound will rally to $2.10 before weakening to $1.50 next year."

This is what I call a 'zig-zag' forecast. Not content to just predict the next price move, the guy thinks he can predict the next two moves. He thinks he has the price on a string. A very untrustworthy type of forecast.

"Upward movement in the dollar will depend on whether the Fed lends a hand by signalling the end of rising interest rates."

This is plain wrong. Rising US interest rates are good for the dollar. Sadly, mistakes as simple as this are not uncommon.

"The markets were overheated so a correction was expected."

Hindsight. With comments like these I always wonder who expected the correction. Did they sell at the right time?

"I'm still looking for a positive January for the Australian dollar as it has done very well in four out of five of the last five starts to the year."

Irrelevant. How can anyone print this?

"The market's gone too far."

Often these comments appear after a big move, but as you will see, I am a firm believer that the market often surprises everyone with how far it can go.

"The market's going to 20,000!"

Or to the moon. Beware of the crazy forecaster looking for a publicity stunt. Yes, it does happen. The wildest forecast gets the most press, and fifteen minutes of fame for the forecaster.

So keep a critical mind when you read or hear market comments. Ask yourself these questions:

- Does the commentator have any track record?
- Are they considering all of the factors?
- If they are pointing to influences which have been present for some time, why should they start moving the market now?
- Are they relying on hindsight?
- Are they hedging their bets?

Part of this is to be a sceptic. Who is the writer? Don't listen to ill-informed, ad hoc, one-eyed, overpaid, inexperienced, sensationalist, untested, uncommitted and uninvolved people!

I would have more respect if a commentator was asked something and actually said 'I don't know'. He could then continue 'because of the following...' and you know you're going to get a balanced answer. It's brave to say 'I don't know', especially if you're in a meeting with traders or at a board meeting talking strategy, and everybody wants to hear your opinion. I try to be disciplined enough to admit that it is just too difficult sometimes to have a view.

As an example, at a Home House function before the Iraq war, Prince Charles asked me what was going to happen to the markets and I said "I don't know, it depends on what happens with Iraq, and you'd probably know more about that than I would!" He agreed – somewhat nervously.

1.9 Understand recent history

If the papers and so-called experts are unreliable, how do you ever learn about markets? The answer is that you should start by trying to understand what's happened in the past. I cannot stress this too strongly. A common mistake of all levels of investors is not doing enough homework. Most of my own time on markets has been investigating how prices have behaved in the past. You cannot hope to predict if you do not understand.

I am not suggesting an enormous amount of research. The effort should be in thinking about how prices have reacted to big picture influences in the past few market cycles. This does not require extensive number crunching or time in the library.

Consider the dollar-euro rate. Before I would ever dare to have a view, I would have to understand where it's been and why. In the last few years, the euro has had a whopping range in value of $0.85 to $1.35. The reasons behind the moves include budget deficits, trade balances, interest rates, economic growth and politics. But these are big picture influences - we don't need to delve into anything too obscure. I will give you more help later with some useful ways to track these things.

An inexpensive education

When you are looking back at price moves you can also perform a useful training exercise. Try to imagine how you would have played the market in the past at different times based on the news which was available. How would you have performed? Would you have picked the big moves?

2 | Comparative Advantages

2.0 To outperform the market you need a comparative advantage

After my disastrous foray into the markets with my own money in 1984, I started trading almost reluctantly for my employer, Bankers Trust Australia, two years later. It began as a part-time activity, because my real job at the time was in swaps, for clients. Risk taking (i.e. trading) became a necessity though, since it was not always possible to cover the risk thrown off when we did a transaction. We were mostly involved with interest rates, and sometimes I would have to cover, say, a five year interest rate risk, with three and ten year instruments. So I started to take a view on what would happen to the different parts of the interest rate curve – the yield curve.

Trading fundamentals

My views were based purely on fundamentals. I had no interest in price charts or all the talk in the market about who was buying or selling. I simply talked to economists and made my own opinion. Sometimes there were kinks in the yield curve for no real reason and common sense told me that they'd disappear at some point. Somewhat surprisingly perhaps, my trading started to make good money for the bank. My boss, Jillian Broadbent, gave me a lot of encouragement, so I then started to trade independently of any requirements from the swaps transactions we were doing. This proved a success and in that year trading profits were $14 million. It was a big amount in those days, even in a dealing room. After I made an even bigger profit the following year, I was encouraged to set up a separate business department, called Positioning, to focus purely on trading. So I somewhat reluctantly left the world of swaps and became a trader.

I set up Positioning quickly and hired three or four bright young university graduates to help me, but we really didn't have much to give us any confidence. When I looked around the room, I saw that every other department, including my old swaps area, had some sort of steady income that it could rely on. Positioning was different. We had absolutely no products or customers. Every day we had to scratch around looking for an opportunity somewhere in the markets.

There were also other pressures. The management of the bank at that time were very professional. They expected discipline, logic and explanations for our activities. There were regular meetings where I had to make presentations to explain the business and I was even obliged to give a profit forecast for budget purposes. I couldn't just give a presentation based on 'we are going to buy this and sell that, and hope for the best'.

Everyone needs an edge

So I began to try to identify whatever 'comparative advantage' we might have had. Comparative advantage is consistent with an original concept from basic economic theory. Some know it as *competitive advantage*, but the term comparative advantage is truer to the real source. The idea is that you should be wary of starting a business selling ice cream on a beach if there are hundreds of other sellers already there. To make any impact you would need to have something different, an edge, when compared to others trying to do the same thing. Similarly, in finance, if you don't have a comparative advantage you should not expect to outperform the benchmarks - the stock and property indexes, short term interest rates, etc. If the market goes up 10%, and you don't have an edge, don't expect to make 12%. That's life.

For Positioning, I could point to the successful track record of my own earlier trading as some evidence of a comparative advantage, but I also needed something that suggested repeatable success, so I could argue that the wins I had made weren't just based on luck or one-off opportunities.

The process of being forced to identify a comparative advantage, in retrospect, was the best thing that could have happened to me as a trader. It meant that I never had the temptation or ability to slip into ad hoc gambling in the markets. My trading had to be based on some sort of logic and discipline.

You should also endeavour to have some structure with your trading. If you believe that you have an advantage, be very clear what it is. Write it down. I gradually identified my advantage in trading and risky investments over the years as these 100 Strategies.

2.1 Everybody is a hero in a bull market!

Psychologists have identified that it is human nature to attribute our wins to our skill, and our losses to our bad luck. Don't fall for this trap.

With trading and investment, luck often parades as skill, especially when a market's doing well. During a bullish run in the stock market you will often meet someone who is very happy with their ability to pick the right stocks, because they have backed one that has performed well. Before deciding to buy, they may have looked very closely at the specific story behind the stock. It is then very satisfying for them to make a tidy profit, and who can blame them for feeling good about themselves. But in the same way that a rising tide lifts all boats, even the rusty ones, many stocks do well in a bull market, even if they're nothing special. So the profit may have more to do with favourable big picture events at the time, such as a strong economy or falling interest rates, than with anything company specific. This really means that the person was lucky rather than skilful.

Now some luck is fine, as long as the recipient doesn't suddenly think they're Warren Buffett and expect to keep backing the winners. I saw a lot of that during the boom before the tech wreck. People trading on the internet backed a few winners in a rising market and became more and more confident about their ability. This led their friends - who heard of their success - to start trading as well. They all ignored the old chestnut that 'everybody is a hero in a bull market'. As prices went higher and higher, they increased their investment sizes, so that when the crash came they had far more money at risk than they would have imagined just a year earlier. It ended badly. Profits tempted them in, and losses forced them out.

Don't mistake luck for brains

So if you back a winner, before getting carried away ask yourself: did I have a real advantage or was my success just caused by something I didn't really understand or predict? If it was purely good luck, you should probably just thank the stars above, and not expect to repeat it.

This applies to all markets, not just the stock market. My first success with trading was in the bond markets, and I used to wonder if it was just luck. I had backed some great trends in interest rates and made good money for my employer, but it was still possible that I didn't really understand what was going on, and that while I had been right with the trade, I could have been wrong with the reasoning. This would not have been a good basis for future success, so I tried to keep my feet on the ground and not get overconfident.

2.2 Never stray from your comparative advantages

In 1995, I left Australia and headed to Bermuda to run a private hedge fund. I had spent ten years at Bankers Trust Australia, so it was sad to leave, particularly as I was leaving nearly all of my team behind, and we were a close unit. Bankers had been an incredible place to work. The people that I had worked for, Jillian Broadbent and later Bruce Hogan, I respect and admire to this day. They are both fun and intellectual, and they backed me when it wasn't clear if I had any ability.

Going to Bermuda was a great opportunity for me to manage a large amount of capital and to be properly rewarded for it. I ended up spending a couple of years there and found it very enjoyable.

Bermuda is one of the most isolated countries in the world, situated all alone in the North Atlantic Ocean. It's only about 50 square kilometres in size, but a surrounding reef protects the island like a fortress. The place has an amazing history, with stories of pirates and adventure that capture your imagination. It's a stunningly beautiful place, with sand that is famously pink, and water that is bluer than blue. The houses add to the colour with an outrageous display of pinks, purples, crimsons and more, but the kaleidoscope works. White limestone roofs everywhere lend a uniformity and prettiness.

On my arrival, it quickly struck me that Bermuda must be one of the quaintest places on earth. 'More British than Britain' was how it felt. With many locals, social formalities are followed to the extreme, often wearing Bermuda shorts of bright colours accompanied by equally bright long socks!

However, not everyone there is content with the status quo. A racial mix of about 60% blacks and close to 40% whites, has seen some debate about who's got what and why. Perhaps this is behind a strong feeling in Bermuda towards gaining independence from Britain. At present, the country is an overseas territory of the UK, with self-government. In 1995 there was a referendum over independence which failed, but there is always talk of another try.

As an Aussie, I can understand the people wanting their own identity and a desire to break free! However, independence could be costly. Bermuda has achieved an extraordinary standard of living under Britain. It has one of the highest incomes per head in the world, despite a lack of natural resources, a tiny population of about 65,000 and little industry. There's also very little soil or fresh water. But they have sailed through on two key industries: tourism and financial services.

Bermuda's comparative advantage

For financial services, such as reinsurance and fund management, the formal link with Britain has offered a strong comparative advantage. Billions of dollars are parked there. For the fund managers and reinsurers, the link with Britain is a huge comfort. If that is taken away, some of the people and money could leave. While this could give the satisfaction of lowering housing prices, it could also seriously hurt the job market. Giving up a comparative advantage could be a high price to pay for national pride.

For investors to stray from their comparative advantages can also be foolhardy. I have had success over the years by being disciplined and applying what I believe are strong comparative advantages. But occasionally I have allowed myself to stray away from using these advantages, and to do silly trades or investments where I have no advantage. This sometimes happens after a particularly good run of profits and I've felt overconfident. It is very, very easy to do and is probably how I ended up with a very strange asset.

Call me Mr Sapphire

In a bank vault in Grand Rapids, Michigan I have possibly the world's largest private sapphire collection! Somehow I've ended up with about 180 kilograms (or 400 pounds) of these stones. Apparently the total is one million carats. Now that may sound exciting, as images of big glistening colourful gemstones come to mind, but it's not as good as it sounds. They may be worthless.

In 1997 I financed a $1 million purchase of the uncut sapphires from Sri Lanka. They were shipped to America for a sapphire exploration company, Gem River Corporation, to heat them and organise for them to be cut and polished. It is a common practice to apply immense heat to raw sapphires, as it finishes the natural process of bringing out brilliant colours. But, for some reason, Gem River was unable to heat them successfully, although they apparently tried. The company had many other issues and soon it went broke. That left me with the stones.

And 'stones' is the right word. I have lots of different colours, including blue, yellow, pink, green and even red (these sapphires are of course rubies), but uncut sapphires are not particularly pretty. They look like small pieces of broken glass with smooth edges.

Eight years later, I still have no idea what to do with them. It's not easy as they live in the States and I'm in Europe. It's a major hassle to even visit them. But the biggest problem is that there doesn't seem to be a market for a big volume of unheated sapphires. From what I understand, most of the dealing is done with small numbers. A lot of it happens in Bangkok, where traders deal in a very small number at a time, and the deals are done between old salts who've been in the business for generations. They use tiny ovens and treat one or two stones at a time, in an overnight process.

I can't imagine rocking into Bangkok with two to three times my body weight in sapphires, and trying to sell them or get them heated. I think the local sapphire dealers might spot an opportunity!

A few years ago I tried to at least find out if they were worth anything, and I arranged for an expert from LA to meet me in Michigan. For a $10,000 fee he was able to give an estimate of between $300,000 and $3 million. My heart picked up – that is until he told me that the stones would look fantastic as rubble in a big fish tank! I'm still not sure if they are worth anything.

So you'd probably class this as an investment gone wrong.

I look back now on this sapphire deal as a clear example of where I strayed from any comparative advantage. At that time I had just started to make some good returns from investments in small companies. I had been right about the strong share market and I had correctly picked the tech sector as an exciting big picture story. I had also identified that small companies often need to raise money at a discount to their fair value, and that I could rate the quality of opportunities largely based on the quality of the management. In retrospect, this success made me overconfident. The sapphires had nothing to do with any of that, particularly as I made no effort to assess the management. I also didn't ask myself why the deal had come my way or why it had been rejected by other potential investors.

So, having very clearly identified your comparative advantage, you must continually remain certain that all trades and risky investments fit the criteria. Continually filter every decision with that in mind.

2.3 A small percentage advantage is enough to outperform the market

A comparative advantage in the markets that is only worth a few per cent can still bring very good results. This will be critical when we look at trading methods that have historically had a small, but lasting, advantage.

Casinos rely on a very small percentage advantage when customers play roulette or other games. On average, I think they will win up to 55%, to the customers' 45%. It's that sort of ratio. It's not a big percentage advantage, but they still make a huge amount of money over time, with enough people betting against them.

Interestingly the only Achilles heel for casinos is when card counters take them on at blackjack. I used to have some fun doing this, and it reinforced my belief in small advantages winning through over a period of time. Card counters are able to track the ratio of high-number cards to low-number cards left in the pack. They can then obtain a very small percentage advantage that can win in the long term. It is not really as easy as it was in the movie *Rain Man*, where Dustin Hoffman's character went to the casino and won a lot in one go. That is not what you expect because the situation is similar to the financial markets, where you can't win with just a few bets, but you can try to win over time.

On one occasion I went gambling with a mate of mine, Berger, and we took equal amounts of money to 'invest'. We spent an entire weekend sitting together playing blackjack, and we didn't get much sleep.

While we were playing Berger would usually ask my advice on the count before making his decisions. He had a pretty easy time of it having more than a few drinks, but I have to concentrate quite hard when I'm counting, so there were no drinks for me. However, Berger did play a role in the whole thing.

He's a bit of a character, and would occasionally completely ignore my count, and just say "what the hell!", as he took a card when he shouldn't, or as he suddenly tripled the size of his usual bet. This caused him some losses, but it had the effect of puzzling the croupiers, who apparently didn't spot my card counting. If they had, they probably would have banned us from playing, since casinos don't like card counters, for obvious reasons.

Anyway, over the three days we won a lot and lost a lot, but there was a steady upward trend and by the end of the weekend we had both made five times our initial stake. Berger thanked me by paying for a nice dinner.

So a small percentage edge is enough to win, if you get enough different trials. It may take longer than a weekend to do it with financial investments, but at least you won't risk being banned.

2.4 Test the advantage over time and make changes slowly

Let's assume that after having read this far you believe that you have a comparative advantage, and you venture forth and start risk-taking. Unfortunately you get hit with three bad losses in a row. What do you do? Keep trying the same thing, give up or try something else?

Since we are only working on percentages we have to learn to deal with randomness. If a casino suffers a big loss on one roulette roll, it doesn't give up. It stays there and stays there and stays there, because in the long run – after banning the card counters - it will win. Despite having identified a good trading technique in the market, you too may still suffer frequent losses. It may just be due to simple bad luck, despite the odds being in your favour. You have to get used to it. These losses will rock your confidence and make you want to give up or try some other technique. However, you really must give the technique a chance to work and not make quick judgements. Later we will look at managing your capital so that you can stay in the game long enough to be able to make a sensible decision about your technique.

Quick success can also be dangerous. Don't get overconfident after just a few big wins. You may have just been lucky, which is not a good basis for increasing your risk-taking or for getting overconfident. For this reason, when I hired new traders, I usually preferred that in their early days they started with small losses. It would teach them discipline and patience, and not to get too carried away.

2.5 Financial markets advantage #1: Information

In searching scientifically for a comparative advantage to make money in the markets, I spent a lot of time considering the advantages that other market participants may use. I was able to come up with four different types:

1. Information

2. Original analysis

3. Brokers and bankers have extra information and free insurance

4. Understanding market behaviour

If you think you have an advantage it will be from one of those four. If it isn't, I would like to hear about it, but be careful, because your comparative advantage probably doesn't exist!

This, and the following three sections, deal with the four types of financial market advantage.

The first type of advantage is the most obvious one: information. It is completely legal and ethical to use many sorts of information, and I know there are many people out there making money with this advantage.

In the financial markets there are continual announcements by companies and government authorities, which often contain a great deal of detail. Examples include company results and official statements regarding interest rate policy. They are often awaited with great anticipation by the markets and scrutinised by analysts worldwide. Just think how many people around the world analyse the statements by the chairman of the US Federal Reserve, Dr. Ben Bernanke.

Face to face meetings are important

There is no substitute for face to face meetings with the important people behind public announcements. At these meetings, it is possible to clarify the meanings of the announcements and to read the body language. For this reason, currency and interest rate traders love to get close to central banks and other officials involved with policy making. Colleagues and I used to visit authorities such as the German central bank, the Bundesbank, to talk to them about their policy. You are always going to get a bit more information by talking directly to the people in control, rather than just reading the newspapers.

We also used to visit fund mangers and we would get a feel for whether they were about to, say, buy dollar assets or European assets. This sort of information can tell you how people are thinking out in the market place. That can be another form of information advantage.

Apart from face to face meetings, there is also the availability of useful public information. For example, during the SARS outbreak, airline stock prices were particularly weak as the market worried about the threat to tourism; a good strategy here might have been to investigate the opinion of the World Health Organisation, and take a view on whether the markets were overreacting. If so, perhaps you would have bought those stocks looking for a bounce.

Information can come quite easily. As a flippant example, it has been suggested that household shoppers have ready access to special information. I bought an Apple iPod music player soon after its release and I was very impressed, so maybe I should have bought shares in Apple. Since I used this consumer electronic myself, I could probably have tested it just as well as any analyst. In that way, someone just doing their shopping could obtain extra information to use to their advantage.

Insider information

Let me stress that the information advantage I've discussed does not involve inside information or anything else of an illegal nature. I will say this though: there is still a hell of a lot of insider trading around. I even met a broker once who admitted "I never buy a stock unless I know something"! Often the price action of a stock clearly reflects insider trading – the price moves, and the reason is revealed later when the company makes a positive or negative announcement. This disease is pretty rife and there are always whispers and rumours.

Personally, I am too paranoid about going anywhere near insider trading – there is just too much risk – because all my business and my personal life have been conducted in the right way. I also find it unethical. So I avoid insider tips like the plague, but even from my remote involvement in different companies, I frequently see and hear about insider trading and I think more should be done to prevent it.

2.6 Financial markets advantage #2: Original analysis

I believe that in the markets there is still a return from doing your homework. This applies to all asset classes: stocks, bonds, commodities, currencies and property. In the share market, if you do some research on companies, such as make comparisons and look at financial data, you may still find that stock-picking can work. This may be especially true for investments in smaller companies.

That original analysis can be of great value is demonstrated by the fantastic track records of a number of funds and analysts. Using the same information that is available to everyone, they are superior in their stock-picking.

The continual improvements in computer power have made many forms of market analysis far easier. With computers people can build sophisticated models to look at all sorts of available information and their impacts on prices. Nothing is too detailed or laborious for the silicon chip!

Even if you don't do this kind of work yourself, you can still get access to other people's fancy analysis. I regularly used to chat to top economists, which was very useful because they do a lot of homework, especially economic modelling and market modelling which are not broadly available to the market. There are also many market newsletters which can give access to high quality analysis.

Over the years I have certainly done my fair share of original analysis. By examining a mass of historical market data I developed a successful trading system that I will discuss later. I have also occasionally gone into some depth when looking at investments in some small companies.

In general though, I personally don't really look to use sophisticated analysis as an advantage in the markets. I am not always convinced about the importance of minute details and I also find them rather tedious. As we will see, I am more interested in big picture ideas and in market behaviour.

2.7 Financial markets advantage #3: Brokers and bankers have extra information and free insurance

When I worked in a dealing room I was always somewhat envious of my colleagues working on the currency and bond desks. Sometimes they had it so easy. They often had a good feel for what their big clients were thinking, and it was extremely useful for them, especially for having an idea of where the market was going over the next day or two. If you have many clients telling you that they are bullish about something, it can be a good signal that you should perhaps buy some yourself!

Information from the order book

The 'order book' can also be very useful. It is extremely common for clients to leave orders to buy a currency or bond a little below the current price, or to sell a little above. The bank will then 'work the order'. These orders can provide a lot of information. At any time, the banker can look at his order book and see the buy or sell orders waiting to be executed at different prices. Now what would you do, if you were a banker looking at his book and seeing a great number of buy orders near the current price, but only a few sell orders? Seeing all of this demand and little supply, you would buy. It is the same for a broker who may cut their position if they start to see sell orders coming in on a stock that they own. In these ways bankers and brokers are able to use the information from their order books.

Free insurance

Order books can also provide free insurance, because market prices often gap. This frequently happens after news announcements. A stock trading at 100 may be hit by news that makes it fall quickly to 90, and there is little opportunity for most players to cut a position along the way; the move just happens so fast. But there can be for a broker. Any buy orders he has sitting on his books can be transacted, and he may have orders to buy at 98, 96, 95 etc. A broker who owned the stock and saw it falling could sell to a client who has left a buy order. This is where we see free insurance.

The information and insurance provided by order books can make good profits. Having worked in dealing rooms for a long time, I know this happens every day, every minute in financial markets, and for that reason I have always been reluctant to leave big orders with banks or brokers! Fortunately, it is getting better for clients as the authorities are pushing for fairer treatment on their behalf.

Few of us are in a position where we have order books and clients, and I will not be pursuing this comparative advantage in the rest of these laws.

2.8 Financial markets advantage #4: Understanding market behaviour

The final comparative advantage arises from an understanding of how the market typically reacts in certain situations. Unlike the information or analysis advantages, this advantage is extremely powerful because it is repeatable. By definition, it is not a singular event but part of an ongoing pattern.

I have stressed that markets are very efficient in setting prices, but there are some inefficiencies which remain, and if you can discover them, you can benefit from them.

Some of the inefficiencies may be fairly straightforward. For example, here are some ideas on the share market that I have read about recently:

- It has been found that companies that list on the share market generally underperform in their early years. If you were trying to use that finding, you could sell out of those new companies and shift into other stocks.

- A flurry of new listings (IPOs) and mergers is known to signal the top of share markets. So if you see a lot of that activity, you would reduce your share positions.

- While analysts are focused on companies' price-earnings ratios, in actual fact, price-sales ratios are a better indicator of future price performance.

- Companies that get more media coverage typically underperform the market in the period after the coverage. (Yet another reason to be wary when you watch those business shows!)

The market opportunity research industry

There are many of these examples and some are not as straightforward. These are discovered by extensive research, perhaps by teams using PhDs in mathematics, statistics or economics. Teams may be set up like machines to find the slightest possible wrinkle in the world markets, and they look at all sorts of different ideas and relationships using massive computer power. Implementation can require huge amounts of capital, instant communication and 24 hour operations.

However, for most types of opportunities arising from market behaviour, the more that people take advantage of them the more they are eliminated. These temporary opportunities are not things I'm recommending for people to research for trading and investment. While my ideas are also based on market behaviour, hopefully they are more sustainable. They are broadly outlined in the next Strategy.

2.9 The Strategies are based on six types of market behaviour

We have seen that I have classified peoples' ability to outperform markets into four comparative advantages. Of the four, the advantage that has always interested me the most, is the understanding of market behaviour. The other three we can give up on. Having access to special information relies on one-offs, and is increasingly questionable. Outsmarting the rest of the market by superior analysis is extremely difficult, and running an order book is only available to banks and brokers. On the other hand, an understanding of the market has offered me a relatively simple and consistent edge for a long time, and I believe this advantage is sustainable. Six key themes are the basis for these Strategies. They are:

1. There remain patterns and anomalies in the markets.
2. Markets are slow to react to structural influences.
3. Small companies offer more opportunities.
4. Markets go further than generally expected.
5. Markets move in underlying trends.
6. A view on the fundamentals can be combined with price movements to manage trading positions.

These six advantages are dealt with in chapters 4.0 to 9.0. Firstly, however, we must talk about a difficult subject: risk.

3 | Risk

3.0 Manage and embrace risk

Learning to deal with risk and losses

I had been trading for a number of years before I learnt how to deal with risk. By solidly identifying some market opportunities I had achieved good results, but I treated finance as a game of chess, an exact discipline, where I expected to benefit from good decisions and suffer from poor ones.

This overambitious approach occasionally caused some bad habits. For instance, when I was not performing well, I made three basic mistakes:

1. I let losing positions drag on for longer than I should, as I hoped that eventually, I would be proved right.
2. I was a bit harsh on myself, and I assumed that to make a loss, I must have missed something obvious.
3. I let it depress me that many hours of work on research and analysis could actually lead to failure.

Equally, when I made profits, I was overambitious and assumed that my reasoning had been right. I thought I was a hero!

Backgammon rather than chess

Fortunately, it didn't take long before I evolved a different way of thinking. I realised that luck plays a role in the investment world. Profits can be simply due to good luck, and losses simply due to bad luck. Financial markets are more like a game of backgammon than a game of chess, because unpredictable events in the markets simulate the involvement of the dice.

With this discovery I started treating markets as partly random and accepted that there was always going to be risk. There is no perfect investment or trade. This approach helped my trading enormously.

- I stopped blocking the possibility of losses out of my mind like some dark fear, and I began to consciously anticipate them.

- I accepted that it would not always be possible to find a reason for a trade going wrong, apart from just chance. So I gave up over-analysing losses with endless post-mortems looking for my mistakes.

- I learnt to assess risks and look at factors like correlation and liquidity.

- Having consciously recognised risk, I reasoned that it was not always a good idea to try and minimise it. I knew that having identified some comparative advantages, I had to trust them to work over time.

- I accepted that even good ideas can lose money. That helped me to get better at cutting losing positions. Being wrong did not mean that I was a lousy trader. Even a trader with a comparative advantage will often make what is later found to be the wrong decision.

This attitude to risk is worth adopting. Accept that trading is unique - a doctor or a lawyer would quickly be out of business with the number of failures that are part of a trader's life.

3.1 Good ideas can lose money

In 1999 and early 2000, Warren Buffett was very sceptical about the rising valuations in the stock market, particularly those in the tech sector. Consequently, he didn't invest as aggressively as many other fund managers. Then, of course, in mid 2000 the share prices of many tech stocks collapsed to a fraction of their boom value. It was a massive market crash, and the so-called 'Sage of Omaha' was proved right (yet again!). I'm sure, however, that even he must have felt some pressure when prices were relentlessly rising and his funds were underperforming. With his reputation though, his investors stuck with him through this difficult period, and he held firm. They believed that he had the right approach, even though he was not getting immediate results.

Be philosophical

In the early days of my career, I used to find it very frustrating when I backed ideas that didn't work out the way I hoped. I took it as a sign that my ideas where flawed in the first place. Today, I'm a lot more philosophical.

In the late 1990s I invested in two companies which I thought had a great future: Addavita and MathEngine.

Addavita – algae production

Addavita was a company with interesting technology for use in algae production. Algae are a primary feedstock for fish, and their production is important for fish farming. With Liverpool John Moores University, Addavita developed units for cost-efficiently growing algae. The units were to be situated on-site at the farms.

Depletion of natural fish stocks in Europe has meant more and more reliance on fish farming, but there has been controversy in recent years about the health effects for people eating farmed fish. As I understand it, because farmed fish eat different food to those in the wild, they can be a different colour, so they are often given chemical supplements to make them look more natural. Another benefit Addavita offered to customers was that they could produce strains of algae which could be used as completely natural colouring agents.

MathEngine – computer graphics

MathEngine's idea was to help produce realistic graphics for the computer games industry. In the mid 90s games were not very lifelike. One problem was that moving objects did not always follow real physics – the equations involved were often too complicated for games programmers. So MathEngine hired university graduates in physics and mathematics who created tool kits for programmers to use. With the use of the tools, phenomena such as bouncing balls, rippling water or shattering glass could be made more realistic.

With both of these investments, however, I lost my entire stake when the companies went broke!

Despite the best efforts of the companies' management teams, they struggled to achieve acceptance from customers. It seems that neither fish farmers nor games programmers wanted to adopt the respective products. This is often the case with new technology, as it is always a battle to get people to do things differently.

Now of course I have asked myself, were these silly investments? But I think the answer is negative. I think that my reasoning was sound, and that the risk-reward when I invested was very attractive. So I put the losses down to probability, and to 'you win some and you lose some'. Both of these investments could have done very well and paid big multiples of the amounts invested. This has happened when I have invested in other companies which were of similar quality in their early days.

Analysis after a loss

If you've lost money on an investment, ask yourself questions such as:

- Were you pursuing a genuine opportunity?
- Did you understand how the market usually works?
- Did you back a big idea or market anomaly that you had identified?
- Was the potential reward worth the risk?

If you have let yourself down, learn from the experience and try not to do it again. But if the investment looks like it made sense, then try not to be put off. Accept that you cannot judge the quality of a single trade or investment by whether you made a profit or loss.

This approach is very disciplined. You do not want to change your investment style on the back of just a few disappointments.

> *The outcome of an investment or trade is not necessarily a true reflection of the merits of the original idea. Good ideas can lose money.*

3.2 Asymmetry has fooled a lot of investors

If an investment opportunity looks too easy, it's time to smell a rat.

There are many types of investment which pay above market returns. The problem is that every now and then there can be a big crash which can take away the profits and cause losses. These types of investments can give the illusion of being very comfortable when they are doing well. However, there is an asymmetry, because most years they will pay-off, but in a bad year they can be horrendous.

Is the higher return worth the risk?

The man in the street may be tempted to chase that little bit of extra return on his investments. Perhaps he may put his life savings into savings schemes such as life assurance or precipice bonds because they pay slightly more than ordinary bank deposits. However these types of deposits are a little bit more risky. Every now and then they can blow up. It's always sad when it's reported on the evening news, that small investors have lost their savings that way. For this reason, I think schools should teach some of the simple principles of investing and probability, not just the highbrow economics.

Professionals can get it wrong as well

It is not just the amateurs that fall for asymmetric investments. Professional bond investors may choose corporate bonds over government bonds because companies pay one or two per cent more yield than the government. This extra margin can look like easy money. Why put your money into government bonds when company XYZ, a solid name, will give you a bit more? But occasionally even good companies fail, and investors can lose 100% of their investment.

Currency markets are often asymmetric, and this has caused some financial disasters. In the 1980s many Australian companies were borrowing in Japan. At that time Aussie rates were cripplingly high, and it was a natural temptation to borrow in Japanese yen to save a few per cent per annum, and to convert the yen into Aussie dollars. This looked like a comfortable existence, which somehow exploited a market inefficiency.

However, the Australian dollar had been chronically weak and, in fact, the market was correctly anticipating further falls. When the Aussie dollar did crash, the cost of repaying these loans soared as the repayments were now much more expensive. The companies' incomes were in Aussie dollars, so it was a disaster for them. There were court cases as they tried to blame the banks who had organised the loans. A bit unfair, I thought, since finance guys working in the companies are supposed to be experts, and they should have known about the risks.

I have even seen high powered traders fall for asymmetric risks. Back before the introduction of the euro, one group I knew at an investment bank were earning great annual bonuses by exploiting the different interest rates in the European countries at the time. They simply borrowed funds in low yield currencies and invested them in high yield currencies. Money for jam! But it was the same deal. They made profits for a few years and then currency moves wiped them out - they lost more than a hundred million dollars. It was interesting to watch. Although they lost their jobs, they of course kept their big bonuses from the earlier years, and they moved on to other employers. Their careers were not even tarnished, because the investment bank was happy to keep quiet about its embarrassing losses. Strange things can happen in the world of finance.

You may not be as lucky as these traders, so be wary of opportunities which make an above average return but can involve high risks. Although they may work for a while, they can suddenly blow up. A smelly rat may come out of hiding!

3.3 Wild swings and losses are uncomfortable, but they may offer the best rewards

While the markets have evolved and become increasingly sophisticated, there has been enormous scrutiny of just about every possible opportunity. Any obvious and reliable way to make money has now probably disappeared.

This means that there are fewer opportunities which offer smooth above-average returns. In fact, the opportunities likely to last longest are those which are the most uncomfortable. Would you be prepared to back an idea that would probably lose money eleven months out of twelve, even if it would probably pay off in the other month? A lot of traders don't want that life. A lot of funds would be hammered with capital withdrawals by their investors. We live in a quarterly or annual reporting world. People evaluate performance over a given period and take action if results are not up to scratch.

By careful management of risk, however, you may be able to take on these uncomfortable types of investments. In the mid 1990s, I had 'retired' and I only wanted to invest my own money. I continued to trade currencies and futures on my own account, and I also decided to start investing in early-stage companies.

Early-stage companies are often private companies which are not listed on any share market, although that is normally their aspiration. There are many of these little unlisted companies searching for financial backers, and they usually find it very difficult, since few investors are interested in them.

Opportunities may be found in areas that others find uncomfortable

One of my reasons for moving into this high risk sector, was that many people find the risk profile too uncomfortable. The majority of the companies fail, and the investor needs to select his investments extremely carefully, and trust that the winners will more than compensate for the losers. Investors also have very little liquidity, and they may have to wait years for a chance to get some money back when the company floats on the share market or is acquired by another company.

This is why I came to the conclusion that good, small companies can be underpriced. This can be an advantage for anyone investing in start-ups if they are able to sort through the many companies looking for money and to choose the good over the bad. I have found the process is not that different to looking at the fundamentals driving currencies, interest rates or other markets, and over a ten year period, I have managed to achieve well over a 20% annual return despite the market collapse in 2000.

Not everyone though, can invest in unlisted companies. The minimum investment needed is at least 50 grand, and you probably need a network to make the introduction. However, I have also been able to apply the experience I have gained from dealing with unlisted companies to help me evaluate small companies which are already listed on the share market. These are accessible to all investors. In a later chapter I will explore the fundamentals of small companies which I think are important for investors to assess. The small listed companies are also generally riskier than the big solid blue chip stocks, but by making an effort to investigate these opportunities and by managing your risk, you may find that these more uncomfortable investments offer a better price.

In general, keep a lookout for investments and trading styles that others don't like. It is logical that it may be here that you find the winners.

3.4 Diversify

The benefits of diversification are very well-known. There is a famous expression saying that diversification is the one 'free lunch' for the investor. No collection of strategies would be complete without a mention of this easy meal.

The world is risk averse. People want to avoid nasty surprises. Investors would prefer to have steady reliable returns, rather than potential wild swings of wins and losses.

Diversification can allow investors to reduce their risk without reducing their overall return. The idea of diversification is that it smoothes out the flow of wins and losses. It is unlikely that a variety of separate trading ideas will all win or lose at the same time. So even if we are placing riskier trades, it may not result in a riskier total portfolio.

I have discussed how I believe that uncomfortable trades with the big swings in wins and losses may offer the best rewards. So diversification is especially useful, because it may be possible to have a more comfortable existence, and still pocket the high return.

There are a few points to note about diversification:

- You can diversify within an asset class. For example, a stock portfolio can have a mix of some blue chips with some small stocks.
- Diversification across all asset classes (stocks, bonds, cash, gold, property etc.) is more effective though, since the positions are less correlated.
- You shouldn't keep a losing position simply because another one is doing well. I was once very sloppy with a losing currency position, because I had a bond position that was profitable, and in aggregate I wasn't losing money. I realised later, that had I used my usual discipline I would have cut the losing position and been much better off.
- Every position in the portfolio should be based on its own merits.
- Remember that you can keep cash as one component in a diversified portfolio.
- Diversification is not an exact science. We will see in the next Strategy that it is difficult to accurately measure risk, so for diversification a rough mix, based on instincts, is probably adequate.

3.5 Assess risk - and then double it

Unfortunately there have been many cases where individual traders, or even entire funds, have 'blown up'. They have been hit by losses so big that they find themselves without a job or a business. In every case the reason is the same: they have not managed their risk. I want to avoid this, and so should you.

For good risk management, the most important thing for me is to always have a rough idea of how much money I could lose if the markets move against me, and I should be able to withstand that loss if necessary.

Risk assessment is not always an exact science

I normally start by going through each of my positions one at a time. Usually, judging how much a position can move against me will be nothing more than a gut feeling. It is difficult to be more scientific about it because:

- Using history as a guide is not always effective, as the world is always changing. I bought stocks after the Iraq war because I thought that they were underpriced and they had an upward trend, but I did not really have any previous examples of what could happen.

- Even in normal conditions, there is a lot of 'volatility of volatility', as the market goes through quiet and crazy periods.

- In many cases the size of the theoretical maximum loss is all of the investment, because a price can go to zero. But it's not much use because we hardly expect that to happen during the time we are involved.

- Sophisticated statistical analysis has often proved inadequate, which is why some high profile names have come unstuck.

My estimate of my maximum loss for each position is therefore based on what I feel could happen in a normal environment. Let's say a normal environment is one which applies four years out of every five.

As an example, I usually assume for risk purposes that blue chip stocks will not fall by more than 25% in four years out of five. So for every $100 I have in the big names, I could expect to lose $25.

Smaller stocks are normally more risky. So, if I invested $100 in a small stock, I may take the view that in four years out of five it would not drop by more than 50%, and I would consider that I was risking $50.

With this estimate for each position, I can simply add them all to get an idea of my total risk. I then have an estimate of how much I could lose in reasonable circumstances - four years out of five. But it could be worse than that. The one bad year in five will happen, so I have to be prepared for an even worse loss. For this reason, I assume I could possibly lose double that amount.

How I assess my total risk

I may however make some deduction if I feel that not everything can go wrong at once. If I have lots of different sorts of positions, and there is some independence in their prices, it would be fair to expect that not all of my rainy days will happen together. This is where you get the benefit from diversification. But be careful, some big name hedge funds have come unstuck by underestimating how much their positions are correlated.

So to summarise, my technique may not be the most elegant, but it is simple and logical:

- for each position, assess how bad a loss could be in a normal environment;
- double the amounts; and
- add up the potential losses, and take some off the total if it is justified by diversification.

The idea is to be comfortable with the total risk level. It is vital that you could withstand that loss, because a disaster may happen. So simply choose the size of positions so that potential losses are manageable. No market is too risky if the position is not too big.

With the right approach you should be able to do what I used to advise traders to do, and that is to "stay in the game". Do not take too much risk.

3.6 Risk adjust results after the trade

Crocodile Dundee is a fantastic movie. It somehow managed to capture the best of the Aussie spirit and sense of humour. A mate of mine was lucky enough to invest in the movie. I think it was the first movie to star Paul Hogan, but even though he was well-known and liked as a comedian in Australia, it was seen as a little bit of a gamble for the investors. When it was finished my mate was invited to see the investors' preview. "I don't think too much of it" was his comment to another investor. The other fellow did like it, and offered to buy him out at his cost price, but my mate thought "Oh well, I've waited this long, I might as well see how it goes". It perhaps wasn't the right reasoning, but it was the right decision. The movie took the world by storm and went on to become one of the top ten earners at the box office up to that time.

What a home run for my mate. Over the next few years his total return was about ten times the money invested, or 1,000%. He wasn't too unhappy!

The thing is though, it was not a great *risk adjusted* return. When I heard this story, I pretty well decided never to invest in movies. The reasoning is that given the high number of movies that completely fail, such a phenomenally successful movie should really pay more than ten times. If you were fortunate enough to invest early in a top ten tech company for example, you would earn maybe a hundred or a thousand times your investment.

Home House experience

I came to the same type of conclusion from my experience with Home House, a London club that I helped to create. When we sold the business in 2004, the price was well above independent valuations, and selling made financial sense. We had created a phenomenal success, as it became very well-known as one of London's leading private members' clubs and it attracted an endless flow of celebrities. However, my return on investment was less than ten per cent per annum. This is not spectacular, because if we had not been successful we could have so easily lost *all* of our investment. So I learnt that the hospitality sector is not really a place to expect to make money. It is probably subsidised by investors who are attracted by the lifestyle it can offer. It *is* fun to walk into your own restaurant or club and hobnob with the customers - but many investors in the sector take a lot of risk and most fail.

The general lesson here is to be critical of even your winning investments and your trading style in general. Did you take a lot of risk to make a profit? Did everything just happen to go your way? Analyse how much risk was involved, and whether the return justified that risk.

3.7 Qualities of the successful trader

When I was first given the responsibility for hiring and firing the members of my own trading teams, I became intrigued with who made good risk takers. If I could figure that out, not only could I hire lots of them, but I might learn something about successful trading. If mathematicians or economists made good traders, the key to trading would probably be in understanding those disciplines. If aggressive or timid people were good, maybe it was because their trading style reflected their personality. I wanted a thumbnail sketch of the 'spectacular speculator'.

For my own part, I always thought that there was nothing to suggest that I'd ever be a good trader. I had never been one of those kids who'd started a little business selling homemade lemonade when I was eight years old. I had no experience with risk-taking of any kind. I did not have the outward confidence that you associate with winners in the markets. Despite all of that, I guess I did have some of the ingredients that contribute to a trader's skill.

Chess hustling proved good training

As a kid I always loved puzzles and games of strategy. When I started playing chess at 12 I had a good aptitude for it, and by 15 I beat the adult state champion in a tournament. Apart from some mental training, this enabled me to make a bit of pocket money, as I used to head off to Hyde Park in Sydney when I could to play chess for money. The people playing were a pretty odd bunch and they'd happily take a few dollars off a 15 year old if they could. But I could usually beat them and I quickly learnt the skill of losing at the right time and of making my winning look lucky, so they'd play for longer and for bigger stakes. Perhaps that can be regarded as a course in risk management and psychology.

Beating adults at chess made me think that perhaps they weren't so bright. With a good memory I drove one biology teacher to distraction when I got into the habit of correcting her mistakes in class about different creatures we were studying. I think I developed an arrogance coupled with a belief that you should figure things out yourself, because so many people make mistakes in their logic.

Throughout my early life though, I was shy and had no self-confidence. I felt like an outsider, which I think originated from the resentment of being taken away from my natural family as a young child. I grew up never really knowing where I came from or where I belonged. I always felt I had to get on with life on my own. I was, at best, very distant from my foster father. I always subconsciously assumed that the closeness of kids to their fathers on television shows like the Brady Bunch, was complete fiction. I had no role model, and no money or connections.

Success was good for me. In my late twenties and thirties I changed so much that I started to enjoy life, and shook off my feelings of inadequacy. So, enough whinging!

I have found that many of my characteristics are present in other successful traders. Drive and ambition are absolutely essential. You won't make it in the financial

> Drive and ambition are absolutely essential. You won't make it in the financial world if you're lazy.

world if you're lazy. I think a disadvantaged childhood gave me my drive and a burning desire to prove that I'm right. I admire those people who come from a comfortable background but still want to achieve something.

The risk-taking elements of trading require self belief and genuine confidence. This is particularly important to handle losses. On the other hand, a big ego is a negative because markets can't be fooled by bravado.

Good traders are almost always aware of the world around them. Many are news junkies and love following the developments in domestic and global politics.

Of course, a good trader needs intelligence and to be practical. Perhaps trading is the ultimate IQ test. I have always thought of intelligence as the ability to sort through a lot of information and to see what is important. I have met many educated and knowledgeable people that I do not think are especially intelligent. The ability to use the information is what they lack. On the other hand, an ability to simplify a complicated subject has always impressed me.

You also need to enjoy what you do. To me, the financial markets are the most exciting experience imaginable. I used to hate leaving the dealing room on a Friday night. At that time, nothing at the weekend could compete with the thrill of the markets.

A level of optimism like this is important. There is a book by Dr. Martin Seligman, *Learned Optimism*, which relates the level of a person's optimism to their success, and even includes an optimism test for readers, which can be revealing. It argues that the most successful people are rational optimists. My interpretation of this relates optimism to an attitude towards risk. Pessimism stops people taking any risk.

But chess players don't normally make good traders

What about logic? Surely that's important for a trader. As a chess player, I have often wondered if other chess players would make good traders. I am very doubtful, because competitive chess players generally live in their own little world. The nature of the game involves sitting opposite an opponent for up to five or six hours with no social contact with them. It would be rude to look straight at your opponent, and you certainly would not speak or smile at them. You need a lot of concentration and calculation, which is great for the brain, but all the information needed is on the 64 squares in front of you, and there is absolutely no randomness. So chess doesn't teach you anything about the real world or the markets. The game does not develop skills in dealing with random events, or to prioritising unfathomable amounts of information.

Strangely, economists don't usually make good traders either, despite them having the best working tools to assess demand and supply, and analyse government policy etc. I find that many of them are not good at assessing odds, and they tend to view markets as somewhat beneath them.

Finally, people sometimes talk about 'burn-out', where traders just become overwhelmed by continual stress. I'm not convinced burn-out really exists. I have seen people stressed by failure who leave the industry, but I have never seen anyone overwhelmed or leave because of success!

3.8 Trading pressure increases with amount at risk

My former boss at Bankers Trust, Bruce Hogan, has a great way of describing how trading pressure increases with the amount at risk. He describes the job as akin to walking a tightrope: it's a lot harder to do the higher you are off the ground.

I've seen many examples over the years, but let me tell you about some lousy trading that I have done, where I broke many of my own Strategies because of the pressure of a big position.

A great flotation but then it all goes wrong

One day in early 2001 I watched the UK stock market open. There it was: ARC International had floated with a valuation of over £1 billion. It was a company I had helped finance as a small company and despite its growth, I still owned over 4%. They produced microprocessor cores which other companies could use in their designs for all sorts of devices, such as mobile telephones. Apart from my pride at helping a company reach a billion, I was obviously ecstatic that my stake was worth a staggering £40 million - I had invested just £3 million into the company a couple of years earlier.

Luckily, I didn't spend the profits. I couldn't take the money out as I had signed a 'lock-in agreement' and was not allowed to sell any shares for six months. The idea of a lock-in is to help the company's shares in their infancy, since you don't want all of the shareholders trying to sell out in a big stampede. When I signed the agreement, I was offered the alternative of selling my shares for around £20 million. I had declined the offer since I knew the market was already valuing them at over £40million and I remember thinking "the market could go down, but not by half in only six months". How wrong I was.

The tech wreck hit the share price hard. ARC was a company that not only had no profits, it had very little revenue. They had a great cash pile that they had raised from investors in the flotation, but they were burning through it with losses as they spent aggressively to gain a foothold with their products. These types of companies very quickly lost favour with the share market.

By the time my lock-in agreement expired and I was free to sell my shares, my stake had declined to about £10 million, still a great uplift from £3 million.

But I went wrong again. I did not sell my shares. I think by then the company's market valuation had dropped below its cash level, and there were rumours that they had signed an important deal with Intel. It all amounted to nothing, as the share price continued to drop like a stone.

I should have followed the Strategies

I should have followed my own Strategies. I am generally against valuation models, and I shouldn't have tried to 'value' ARC at more than the market price on the basis that it had a lot of cash.

Besides, there were many other companies trading on the market at that time below their cash value that were not losing money, and they would have been a better bet anyway. I also had no reason to back ARC's management (Strategy 6.1), and as the price fell it went much further than I expected (Strategy 7.0). My comparative advantage (Strategy 2.0) had also largely disappeared when the company listed. Why did I believe that ARC, a publicly listed company, was worth more than its market price?

In the end, I finally sold my shares in ARC in the first half of 2003 for total proceeds of about £3.5 million. Not a disaster, as I had somehow made a profit of about half a million pounds, but it was a paper loss of over £40 million from the day the company first traded.

When it goes wrong in this way, it is very stressful. I think in the back of my mind, I knew I was doing the wrong thing by not cutting my position, but I was living in hope and ruminating over the past. I kept kicking myself for signing the silly lock-in. I am sure Goldman Sachs, the broker who did the float, would have succeeded with the float of the company even if one shareholder, such as me, had not agreed to sign. They made a big fee, and everyone wanted the float to go ahead. So I had made a series of errors.

> *Under stress, one error leads to another.*

The emotional side of investing must be recognised and controlled

The emotional side of investing is impossible to ignore, particularly if your own money or your career is at stake. I have always tried to remain level-headed whether I've lost money or made money. When the price of ARC was collapsing, I also had many other technology investments. They were all still private companies and hence very illiquid. The price of all of them - when there was a price - was dropping rapidly in the same manner as the ARC share price. It was horrible.

In a market crash, trying to raise money for private companies is close to impossible. Many investors are too busy trying to fix their existing portfolios, and they have no time or money to look at small niche plays. As existing owners of the businesses, you then get these tough requests to put even more money into something which is dropping in value. Your money is needed to keep the business alive, and to protect your existing investment, because no one else is willing to do it. It's not what you want, as it can be good money after bad. You end up investing more in a company than you ever envisaged, because normally your early investment in a small company would be followed by later investments by large funds and venture capitalists, but when they're not interested, it's back to you.

So the tech crash was a nightmare for me. I don't know how much money I lost from the highs but it was probably over £100 million including the ARC drop. It was tough to take as I had started investing in tech in the mid 1990s, way before it had become a fashion for people who really didn't know what they were doing. After six or seven years, I had only needed another six months or so, when a lot of my companies were due to float or be sold at a great return. It was a 90% completed task, which tripped at the last hurdle.

Stress affected my investing

Don't feel sorry for me. I became involved in technology way before it became fashionable and over-hyped, and the profits I made gave me a big buffer when the tech crash arrived. I had taken money out of the market with every opportunity and had made great returns along the way. I always kept enough cash in reserve to maintain my lifestyle so I was luckier than a lot of people, who were really decimated by the fallout. But in retrospect I still showed signs of stress. I forced myself not to complain and to remain outwardly positive on my investments. However, I wasn't sleeping well, I was moody and irritable, I was difficult to get on with and I found it hard to get too interested in other things in life. I played speed chess on the internet for hours on end as a means of escapism.

The lesson is, of course, to know yourself. Are you in too deep? Are you gambling or living on hope? Be critical of yourself and don't blame others or outside circumstances. Don't let one mistake lead to another - or you might fall off the tightrope.

3.9 The trader's dilemma - the stop-loss?

Many traders use 'stop-losses' on losing trades. They decide in advance how much of a loss they are prepared to tolerate on a particular investment or trade. If the market moves against them and reaches a predetermined price, it will be closed and the loss stopped, no matter what. This technique enables an assessment of the potential cost if things go wrong. If they buy a stock at $100 with a stop-loss price of $75, they know in advance that their maximum loss is $25. There are also other variants which aim to limit the potential reversals of profitable positions. With a 'trailing stop-loss', the stop-loss price rises in line with the market price. So if the market rallies by $10 to $110, the stop-loss price might also rise by $10 to $85.

The benefits of a stop-loss are quite clear: It forces an investor to be disciplined. When a position goes wrong it can cause stress and cloud people's judgement. Anticipating this, and deciding on a stop-loss level in a calm and relaxed manner beforehand, can ensure that an investor will remain objective. A stop-loss also allows a specific amount of capital to be allocated to each idea. So an investor might be prepared to lose say, 10 grand on a hunch, and say, 25 grand on a firm conviction.

Despite the advantages, I have never been sure of the stop-loss approach. It doesn't seem very scientific, and I'm not sure it is necessary if the other risk management ideas in this chapter are followed. In fact, I think the choice to cut a losing position is a dilemma. On the one hand, the positives for managing risk and preserving capital are clear. On the other hand, if you are confident a trade is a good idea but the price moves against you, perhaps you should be buying more, or at least holding, rather than cutting.

Certainly one discipline which should be used in any case, is 'marking to market'. You should value your positions at least once a day, and use the current market price. Forget any talk of 'it's only a paper loss until it's sold'. A losing position clearly means that something unexpected has happened.

Over the years I have come to the following conclusion on stop-losses. When you put on a trade, have a stop-loss in your mind. If the trade then hits the stop-loss level, make a judgement on whether to cut, based on your confidence at the time about the position.

If the loss is threatening to be destructive to your finances, it is absolutely vital to cut. To be at this point, the price must have moved a really long way against you, if you have not bet too much on the idea in the first place.

You must also cut if you are confused about what is going on, or if the fundamentals are moving against you. This is consistent with later Strategies where we will see that prices go further than expected, and that they move in trends.

Stopping out is the hardest trade. No one likes to give up hope. But it is essential in these circumstances. Beginner investors should be especially cautious about mounting losses.

Sometimes you cut a position and then the market recovers. Don't be put off stop-losses by those experiences. The horrible feeling of cutting a position only to watch the price turn and recover is one of the worst for a trader. Remember though, we are talking about probability and random events, and over time all sorts of good and bad things will happen. We have got to look at the long term. Normally after cutting a bad position there is a strangely cleansing feeling - some people say it's a bit like getting out of a bad relationship!

The decision not to cut

Having said all of this there are times not to cut a position, even if it reaches your stop-loss level. These are when two conditions are satisfied:

1. you have the capital in case of further losses;
2. you understand the reasons for the adverse price move, but remain confident that there will be a recovery.

Here it may make sense to hold the position and even to consider buying more. (I would still like to see the market starting to recover before I added to a position, but more on that later.)

The decision to keep a losing position must not be based on emotion or on any sense of living in hope. You must admit to yourself that things have not gone the way you expected, and that since you have been wrong up to this point, you may well be wrong again. There is an old saying along the lines of 'the market can remain irrational much longer than you can remain solvent'.

Unwired Group Limited

I had a fortunate experience when I chose not to cut a losing investment in an Australian wireless internet company. In 2000 it had bought data transmission spectrum in the national auction, and it had added to this holding in 2001. Nothing much had happened in the grim tech wreck years, but in 2003, they felt ready to raise money and begin operation. The company was to list by taking over Unwired Group Limited, which trades on the Australian market. They approached me as a private investor.

I get lots of these approaches, but Unwired was a compelling story. The management presented well, with good track records, and I was able to check them out a little via mutual contacts.

The Unwired product would be wireless broadband internet which the customer picks up by purchasing and installing a special modem. The plan was to roll-out in Sydney first, and if successful to add other major cities. It would offer a good alternative to normal land lines, especially to those whose land line was inadequate to carry broadband. The product would be portable, so it could be taken from home to office, and would also be attractive to people who rent accommodation. Installation would not be complicated, and the modem would be sold in shops and by wholesalers. The technology could be complementary to other new technologies, such as 3G mobiles.

The company was raising plenty of cash from a good investor base, which would fund the Sydney roll-out. The cash would be used to buy tower space for the transmitters, inventory of the modems and for a marketing campaign. There was also a solid barrier to entry for potential competitors, through Unwired's ownership of its spectrum. For this reason, it could become a takeover target for big telecoms looking to expand their markets or to prevent a loss of their broadband market share.

So, in December 2003, I invested in the company at an effective price of 90 cents, which implied a market capitalisation of about A$220 million. Over the next six months the price had a strong trend - downwards. In July 2004, it fell to as low as 55 cents.

This was around the stop-loss level I had in mind when I invested.

There didn't seem to be any reason for the dramatic fall. Everything seemed to be going on track for the company. The network was being set up, trials of the system were progressing and the modems they had ordered were being delivered.

Here was a classic stop-loss dilemma. If I had thought that there was any way the price would drop so severely, I would not have invested. The fundamentals were sound, so if anything the company was a buy at this price, rather than a sell.

I held on to my investment. Since I had quite a large position, I didn't buy any more. Fortunately for me, the price recovered as the company achieved some success with its product launch in August 2004 following a strong advertising push. That sent the price to over A$1.10. I later exited my position at around A$1.00, when I became worried about potential competition emerging from other companies.

So with my Unwired position I did not use a stop-loss, and the market recovered allowing me to salvage a small percentage profit. My confidence was rewarded. However, in the previous Strategy, I told of my tough experience with my ARC shares, where cutting a deteriorating position would have been the better choice than hanging on, and where clearly I was stressed and lacked discipline – exactly the problems that a predetermined stop-loss strategy seeks to avoid. So these two episodes feature the pros and cons of using stop-losses.

Summary on stop-losses

With all of this in mind I will repeat my advice: follow the other Strategies in this chapter by not betting too much on one idea and by anticipating market moves twice as big as seem reasonable. Have a stop-loss in your mind when you put on a trade and if the price hits the stop-loss level, *always* cut if:

- the loss is threatening to be destructive;
- you are confused about what is going on; or
- the fundamentals are moving against you.

You should only keep the position and consider increasing it if you remain genuinely confident about the underlying fundamentals. Experience will help you recognise when you are starting to rely on nothing but hope. If you do stay in, choose another stop-loss level as a reference point, and stay disciplined.

Patterns and Anomalies

4.0 Look for patterns and anomalies

In this chapter we start to look for trading ideas. But where will these ideas come from? I have dismissed the so-called experts as not being very useful. There are thousands of different stocks, bonds and commodities. How can an investor find anything?

The first thing you need to do is to **be inquisitive about the markets.** You will probably be drawn to the markets that you find most interesting. As you get to know more, try to identify patterns and anomalies in the way they behave. These will be the basis of your trading ideas.

An inquisitive nature

I have always looked for anomalies in my world. I love to challenge things and this has affected me fundamentally. I was quite a Christian in my teens and was considering the idea of becoming a minister; until I decided that there was no way Judas could have betrayed Jesus. Love or fear would have stopped him, I figured, and after much thought I abandoned religion altogether.

I was also interested in less spiritual things. I found a mischievous way of using out-of-date tickets to travel cheaply on Sydney trains. With international sporting fixtures, I noticed that you seemed to get good odds when betting against the home side, because most people bet for who they want to win, somewhat regardless of the odds.

It was natural that I was equally inquisitive in the financial markets. I had many ideas that evolved into actual trading techniques.

Watch crowd behaviour

I picked up one good idea in Japan. On my frequent visits I noticed that many traders and investors would say the same thing about the markets. This applied to the share market, interest rates and to the yen. It was amazing.

There were no real debates anywhere, they just seemed to follow the herd. When they were wrong, such as in the 1987 share market crash, they were very slow to cut their positions. I guess it is consistent with the stereotype of Japanese society where everyone just wants to conform, and individuality is discouraged. To me, the Japanese behaviour presented an opportunity. By carefully monitoring the local viewpoint, I jumped onto some great trends and jumped off when the Japanese started to turn more neutral. It was a good lesson on how to trade with a consensus, rather than against it.

Think for yourself

Early in my career, I also took advantage of anomalies in the Australian government bond market. In those days, with big budget deficits in Australia, the markets were nervous about the size of government borrowing. So, once a year, on budget night, the market used to wait nervously for the announcement of how much the government expected to borrow over the following twelve months. The popular thinking was that the more borrowing needed, the worse for the bond market, and so the announcement was usually followed by a knee-jerk reaction in bond prices. I reasoned, however, that Australia was a relatively small market in international terms, and a few more bonds for sale would not really affect the demand from foreign buyers. This generally proved right, and I made money from this by betting that most of these reactions were only temporary.

As a trader, you need to keep an open mind. Think about crazy things.

When I was interviewing potential traders, I used to like to test them by asking challenging questions. For example, on a small island, what would happen to the local economy if they discovered a huge gold reserve? What would happen to the markets if scientists found a way for all of us to live forever? It wasn't the answer that the interviewees gave that was important, but the thought processes they revealed.

I am now going to lead you through some ideas that you can implement yourself in the markets. However, you shouldn't stop coming up with your own ideas.

4.1 Choose the right markets

In many cases where you have a view on the economy, or the world in general, there will be different ways to position yourself in the markets. As an example, if I was bullish about the Chinese economy because of the massive growth potential, off the top of my head some ways to invest would be:

- buy Chinese stocks;
- buy into shipping stocks (prices are already much higher on increased Chinese usage for shipping of imports and exports!);
- buy the yuan (the Chinese currency);
- buy commodities (raw materials), looking for Chinese demand to push up prices;
- buy into a currency that exports commodities (e.g. Australia and Canada); or
- buy stocks in foreign companies who will sell products to China, for example mobile phone companies such as Nokia.

I'm sure there are more. I'm not going to unravel this example - without some homework I couldn't even guess the right answer.

I will say this: when you have a view and there are a number of ways to implement it, look at four criteria. Choose the market:

1. Where the price has not already adjusted, or has adjusted the least, to the events you expect. This could rule out shipping, because shipping prices have already moved substantially higher in line with greater Chinese activity.

2. Where there is the least downside risk if you are wrong. If you have more reasons for being bullish on Nokia than just Chinese demand, buying Nokia stock may provide some protection if it turns out that you are wrong about the Chinese.

3. Where there is the least random influences to mess up your idea. The announcement of a government election in Australia, for example, would probably dominate the movement of the A$ up or down, and the Chinese economy would have little short term impact. In the event, the Canadian dollar would be better suited as a currency play on China, until after the election.

4. Where you have the best liquidity. This is the ability to buy and sell easily and inexpensively. Some Chinese stocks may be too illiquid.

Very often, you cannot meet all the criteria and the different criteria steer you towards different markets. It will then be a matter of judgement. What I want to do is get you thinking about various opportunities and the risks they involve.

4.2 The share market dilemma

Strangely enough, I have always been nervous about investing in the share market. Although I have often invested in smaller companies which largely succeed or fail on their own merits, I have mainly stayed away from the big blue chip stocks. One reason is that many years ago I noticed a dilemma and it scared me off.

The dilemma arises because the share market likes profits, but it does not like rising interest rates.

The share market likes profits, because these help pay higher dividends, and increase companies' cash reserves. That's why the market eagerly awaits the earnings seasons when companies announce their results.

The share market doesn't like higher interest rates because they mean higher borrowing costs for businesses. They can also make shares look less attractive than cash deposits.

The problem is that profits and interest rates tend to rise and fall together with the performance of the economy, and so the share market is frequently being hit with good and bad news at the same time.

Because of this share market dilemma, it can be quite difficult to stay with a bull market. Even if you are fortunate enough to buy into the rising market early, you are still likely to be hit with a lot of turbulence in the price. There will be many down days among the up days, as the thought of higher interest rates distracts the market.

Sure, there have been great runs in the market in the 1980s and 1990s, but that had a lot to do with a long run decline in inflation, which helped interest rates to fall even when the economy was doing quite well. If inflation levels out, the normal dilemma will come back.

The share market dilemma is probably most likely at turning points in the economy. This was the case in the early 1990s when the economy was recovering from a recession, and the share market started to rise in anticipation of higher profits. It was a great time to buy stocks, as the market had an unbelievable run for the rest of the decade. However, in line with the dilemma, interest rates started to rise, and there were many down days in the market, which probably shook many traders and investors out of their positions.

A similar thing happened from 2003 to 2005 when the share market performed strongly following economic recovery from the tech wreck and the invasion of Iraq, but again an environment of rising interest rates, particularly for the US markets, caused a lot of down moves as well as up moves. This could have made life tough even for those who were right about the big picture.

I will discuss more about the share market in later Strategies, but the observation here is: if you are bullish on the market, you may be right, but don't expect an easy ride.

4.3 Crisis situations almost always provide an opportunity

I do not like buying into falling markets. I do not believe that the occasional successes will pay for the more numerous failures. Buying falling markets is inconsistent with my basic ideas of how markets work, which include that markets move in trends and that they surprise us by how far they move.

Panics can lead to an imbalance in supply and demand

Nevertheless, I want to discuss an exception: crisis situations. In crisis situations almost anything can happen because there is panic in the markets. I have seen the most controlled and sensible people completely lose all their judgement when they are under intense pressure. Sometimes the whole market is awash with nail-biting traders feeling nervous and confused. With the volatility that we have experienced in the last 25 years, there have been many such episodes. The share market crash of 1987, the emerging market crisis of the late 1990s, the tech wreck, and 9/11 are just a few that come to mind. And, undoubtedly, there will be many more.

The reason that there are opportunities on these occasions is simple: a falling price triggers more panic selling than it does bargain-based buying.

During these crises, many players will be forced to cut their positions regardless of the price. Some funds will have lost so much money on many different investments, that their very survival would be threatened if they lost more. They may reason that by selling, they take a dreadful loss, but at least it does not put them out of business. Even though holding on may be a great trade, they simply cannot take the risk. There have been many instances of a senior manager ordering a fund manager to cut, and ignoring their heartfelt pleas not to do so.

At this point fresh buyers could come into the market looking for value. However, at times like these, potential buyers may be too distracted with their own problems to do anything. This particularly affects smaller markets since fewer people are watching them anyway.

Suffering from this lack of buying, the market could paradoxically be struck by new selling. Some hedge funds and other momentum players may ignore fundamental valuations and see selling as an opportunity, as they look for the price to go even lower. (This type of trading is discussed later in the book.)

While all of this is going on, you may be able to step in. I hope that you will have followed good risk management so that you yourself are not facing a crisis, and you can keep a cool head even as others panic. My advice in that situation, is to be extremely choosy over how you get involved in the market - try to consider many different opportunities and don't necessarily jump at the first one you see. In a genuine crisis, there will be no shortage of ideas.

The tech stock collapse offered opportunity

In the darkest days of the tech crash there was a genuine crisis. Clearly, there had been an unbelievable bubble with crazy prices and a lot of hype. Complete novices were trading tech stocks online. I am sure with the crash, many casual observers thought that tech stocks and tech investors got what they deserved. However, what I did see at the time was that small tech companies were being binned indiscriminately. Along with the silly dot-coms, which had no real products or hopes of revenue, there were some good companies. Some with extremely good management, products and prospects, but in need of capital, were just left to go broke. Sometimes technology that had been developed in the hands of very competent teams over years and at great expense, pretty well disappeared.

At that time, due to the lack of liquidity of some investments in unlisted companies, I was having problems with my own portfolio. However, I had followed good risk management, so I was never forced to sell in a panic, and my lifestyle was not put at any risk. As a known investor in small companies, I was getting an unbelievable number of phone calls and emails from companies looking for emergency money.

So I looked at many opportunities and I ended up being the lead investor rescuing two tech companies which otherwise were due to be shut down. In both cases, the price was very low and a fraction of the price a year earlier.

One went broke very quickly, and I lost the money. It did not get some orders that it needed, and I was not prepared to put a second lot of funds into the business. The other survived and prospered. Two and a half years later, I still have my shares and the price is 500% higher. Of course, some people would say, 'Oh, that's a lucky investment!'

These crisis situations, where there are forced sellers with not many buyers, happen in all markets from time to time, but mostly with smaller stocks, property, and parts of the bond market (mainly the corporate and emerging market bonds). The bigger the market, the less likely there is to be a lack of buyers. Consequently, there are probably fewer crisis opportunities with the currency markets and with larger stocks.

The Strategy does not imply that every difficult situation is an opportunity. Recently I have been asked to participate in another rescue of a company which has run out of money, and lost the confidence of its shareholders. However, it is not a crisis in the general market; it is only a crisis at the company. A number of potential investors have had the time to look at the opportunity and passed it up. It is not that these investors are too preoccupied or scared to invest, they have just decided that the company is not good enough to support. I do not see an opportunity either.

4.4 Short term interest rates will tend toward the inflation rate plus the economic growth rate

I love this Strategy. It is a very good one - even if it is just used in isolation. It may not be exact, but it provides an extremely good starting point.

There is, of course, always a great deal of discussion about interest rates, particularly US rates. Short term rates are set by governments and this can be a fascinating process to watch. The rates affect the economy and many of the markets. The benchmark strategy helps to make sense of discussions about their direction and their level. It is a rough guide which is often missed by many commentators. With this rough valuation target, I have usually found that interest rates are easier to understand than most markets, where it can be hard to have a clue what the price should be. Equities, the market that most investors concentrate on, do not have this kind of benchmark, and do suffer from the dilemma of the share market which I identified earlier.

The basis for the strategy

An interest rate is made up of the inflation rate plus a 'real' rate. That is, the real interest rate is what is left after allowing for inflation.

The economic growth rate is the percentage expansion or contraction in the economy with inflation stripped out. It can be loosely considered as the dividend paid by the economy in general.

In my view, over time the real interest rate moves towards the economic growth rate. In that way, the return from interest rates and the economy in general, are equal.

Currently short term rates in the US are 1%. When they start to rise, how far could they go? My target using this strategy would be about 4%, because inflation is around 2% and growth is also around 2%. Add them and you get my target.

On one occasion I had an interesting debate with an in-house economist. Rates had started moving lower worldwide and he was very cautious about how far they could fall. My view was that they could move much further. I simply used my strategy - nothing more was needed - and was not only proved right, but took some great wins in the bond market as well. The strategy is a gem, a ripper!

4.5 Government bond markets for the major economies are not prone to crashes

Apart from the level of interest rates being somewhat predictable, there is another thing I like about bonds - they are not as risky as stocks. Many people point out that stocks outperform bonds in the long run. Perhaps. However, one comfort you do have with high-grade bonds is that you are unlikely to wake up in the morning and find you have lost 25% of your investment, which of course does happen occasionally with stocks.

Divergent behaviour of stocks and bonds after economic shocks

Most unexpected shocks to the economy are bad news - a crash in consumer or business confidence, a terrorist attack, a war, a SARS crisis etc. Now if one of these pushes the economy into a dive, stocks plummet while bond prices can actually go higher.

I learnt this lesson in 1987 during the October share crash. Panic was all around me. I kept quiet - all I had were bonds and they did very well. The bad news for the economy was good news for interest rates.

It is also interesting to consider the effect of government deficits on bond yields, especially in the United States. One could argue that the government bond markets should work like all markets, so that if the government wants to borrow more and more, it has to pay a higher interest rate, and sell bonds at a lower price. This was a criticism of fiscal policy by one brand of economists - the monetarists. They argued that 'crowding out' would mean that higher deficits don't help a weak economy, because they simply push up borrowing costs for everyone. I am not convinced by this though, and current rates in the US are normal even though the deficit is at an all time high.

I don't want to oversell bonds and scare you away from owning stocks. There have been some dream runs in the share market, and there will be plenty of times when these strategies will steer you in that direction. However, the world to me often seems share-obsessed, and I'm just alerting you to the attractions of a different market.

4.6 Currencies: two economies and fact or fashion?

Currencies are very difficult. Even though I have had good results trading currencies, I have always found them more difficult than stocks and certainly more difficult than interest rates.

I have urged you to learn by looking at price behaviour in the past, but trying to understand what currencies have done even recently is tough. There have been some big moves. Take the US dollar versus euro rate, for example. It has ranged over the last few years from around 85 to 130. How is it possible that the currencies of the world's two largest economies can change in relative value by over 50%?

These types of currency moves have always intrigued me. The first thing to be aware of, is that you are looking at two economies. With stocks and interest rates you basically have only one economy to figure out. However, the second and bigger challenge is that currencies are largely driven by market sentiment, and the reason is that there is absolutely no successful benchmark for the pricing of a currency.

Purchasing price parity is not much use

There is one theory called 'purchasing price parity', PPP, which suggests that currencies should tend towards the level where a collection of goods and services costs the same amount in different countries. PPP would suggest that if they are too expensive in one country, then that country's currency should fall.

The famous McDonald's Big Mac index is sometimes published in the *Economist* magazine, and it applies this analysis, somewhat tongue in cheek, to the price of the burgers in various countries.

The problem is that in reality PPP does not seem to have much impact on currency levels. Perhaps it is for the same reason that people living in tiny but very expensive apartments in Tokyo do not migrate to Sydney or LA and buy a huge house. If they did, perhaps currencies would be easier to evaluate.

Market sentiment has the most impact

Since there are no reliable benchmarks, market sentiment is the huge factor that dominates events. Recently the US dollar has been out of favour, despite an improving US economy and rising US dollar interest rates. The market is more worried about the US current account deficit. But is that economics or fashion? There's the difficulty.

In conclusion, I wouldn't say that you need to avoid currency trading completely. There are the occasional opportunities such as the big market moves that we have seen in the major currencies during the last few years. But I feel that you should only be involved when you have a very firm grip on what's driving the market. That doesn't happen too often for any of us!

4.7 Some markets are driven by supply

The stock and property markets are mostly driven by demand. Housing supply in, say, London, does not change much or do unpredictable things. Therefore, it is the changes in demand that push the prices up or down.

Some markets, however, are supply driven. I have in mind here some commodities (raw materials), especially foods and, to some extent, oil. Consider coffee for example. Unless there is something like a health scare about coffee, the demand around the world remains quite constant, and the main thing affecting the price is the changing supply from producers.

It is important to know if you are involved in a supply driven market, because **these markets are more difficult.** Their price moves are harder to predict, because:

- they can be driven by the vagaries of the weather and the natural environment; and

- in some cases the commodities are coming from developing countries. These may be politically unstable and news flow may be unreliable.

In a later chapter, I will suggest the best times to buy into different markets. When commodities look good as an asset class, I would strongly suggest that you trade a mixture of different commodities. This smooths out the randomness of supply driven markets. Don't let a plague of locusts ruin your big picture trade.

4.8 Property prices often lag stock prices

In 1989, I shocked a lot of people in my dealing room when I suddenly sold my home in Sydney, and put my sale proceeds into Deutschmarks. It was viewed as rather bizarre. However, I was convinced that the property market would start to feel the effects of the share market crash some eighteen months earlier.

I was also very keen to rent a stunning apartment overlooking Sydney Harbour. It was directly opposite the Opera House, and nearly as high as the Sydney Harbour Bridge. Despite having one of the best views in the world (this is an Aussie speaking!) it wasn't actually very expensive - amazingly only a few hundred Aussie dollars a week.

Anyway, as it turned out I was right about housing prices (and fortunately the Deutschmark, which went on to rise against the Australian dollar).

In general, share prices have been a good *leading indicator* for property prices, which often follow the direction that the stock market took two or three years earlier. The economy pushes shares and property in generally the same direction, but with property, the reaction takes longer.

There are always exceptions to rules

Recently however, there may have been a de-coupling of the two markets, and this strategy may not have been very effective.

A few years ago, stocks were dominated by weak global economies and the tech wreck. This was followed by a persistent recovery which started after the invasion of Iraq. Housing prices on the other hand, have until recently been surging, inspired by the massive drop in housing interest rates.

So housing has not shown any tendency to follow a lead set by the share market. But, I am going to keep this Strategy!

It is always valuable to be aware of patterns like this and when they don't work, to try and figure out the reason. On this occasion, dramatic events have dominated each of the markets, and swamped any usual behaviour.

It is not too bad. Remember, we only need these 100 Strategies to be right on most occasions or on our bigger positions, to have a comparative advantage.

In this particular case, you will see later that with the trading style I use, I would not buy or sell property just because of the share market – I would always wait until property prices themselves started to move in the right direction, to give me further confidence.

Property may be the easiest market

I am going to go as far as saying that despite a lot of talk about whether stocks, bonds or cash are the best investment, it may be the property market that is the easiest of the markets, for three reasons.

1.   By following this Strategy, you can watch the stock market for a useful buy or sell indicator, and have plenty of time to act in the property market.

2.   There are not many false trends in property prices. The market is not a listed market where everyone can see the prices – deals are done privately and price trends develop slowly and surely. You can wait for the herd to start to move and then join them for a nice journey.

3.   Just about everywhere there is no tax on capital gains on people's own homes.

4.9 Chartists are the astrologers of the markets

I am sure that you have seen price charts in the newspapers and on the television. They are extremely popular. Chartists believe that they can see patterns in charts which can predict future price movements. They like to superimpose straight lines over the charts, usually connecting a series of high or low points. Sometimes they also have squiggly lines drawn on them as well. The chartists all have their own systems that they follow, normally based on the thoughts of a guru from a long time ago, or perhaps some strange pattern which exists in nature. And the jargon they use sounds very scientific. Expressions such as 'declining wedge' and 'fourth wave' suggest to outsiders that the systems are profound and well researched. The beauty for chartists is that they don't need to know anything about the market they're trading. They have no need to look at fundamentals.

In my quest for looking for patterns and a repeatable methodology, I was obviously aware of chartist theories. Although I love to apply rigour and science to trading, I didn't get distracted by them, and nor should you.

Chartists have no scientific basis

Let me be clear on this: I don't mind having a look at the odd chart every now and then, it's the crazy theories that chartists use that I don't like. Charts themselves are useful for a feeling of how far markets can move and how they react to news flow. However, a few things are obvious about chartist theories. These ideas are not applied in the economics field which is always searching for theories on human behaviour. Nor do the theories have a true mathematical basis, and the chartists that I've met, tellingly, do not have a mathematical background of any kind. Probably worst of all though, is that I don't know any successful chartists - though probability would suggest that there are a few out there somewhere.

I'm also not a big fan of fixed time-frame cycles, which are favoured by some chartists. I don't believe, for example, that markets will peak and trough every x number of years. They may accidentally have formed some pattern in the past, but there is no reason whatsoever that it should continue.

So, I have to be emphatic here: chartists are the astrologers of the markets. They use a pseudo-science. Apart from a somewhat clumsy way of following trends, their methods are unsubstantiated, though extremely popular. There is simply no reason, for example, why price moves should imitate the pattern of plant growth, star patterns or anything else.

5 | Big Ideas

5.0 Markets are slow to react to structural influences

In the early 1990s, I was asked for my view on the Nikkei - the Japanese share market index. I replied that I was in no way optimistic, partly because of the weak banking sector which had too many bad loans. I vividly remember the response: "No, no. That's *old* news." But I was right, and even ten years later, the banking sector's problems persisted, and the Nikkei was dragged lower and lower. The weak banking sector was a structural influence on the Japanese markets, and I don't believe that these things disappear in a hurry. Even the biggest markets in the biggest economies can take a long time to react to the biggest news.

Structural influences

Structural influences are those that are deeply embedded in the system. You might call them 'big picture' fundamentals. They can have a slow but persistent effect on economies. The cheap supply of labour becoming available in India and China has a slow and almost hidden impact on western economies. As a structural influence, it is not likely to disappear overnight, and its effects may be felt for decades.

Structural influences are often phenomena without precedent. When we experienced things like the ending of the Cold War, the onset of information technology, the aging of the western population or the mapping of the human genome, we entered new territory.

Because structural influences are so unique, their effects can be tough to forecast and measure. They are not like normal economic cycles where economists have a host of experience to indicate how far, say, interest rates can rise or fall.

That's why I believe that these big picture influences are generally underestimated in the financial markets. It takes time for these things to be fully priced. If we can identify them and their likely impact, we can find profitable investment opportunities. That is the subject of the next Strategy.

5.1 Look for the next Big Thing

"I give the talkies six months more, at the most a year. Then they're done."

Charlie Chaplin, 1931

This is probably top on the list of my favourite quotes. A woeful prediction by an amazing man! Soon after, silent movies disappeared and sound was a phenomenon in the movie world.

If we can predict the next big thing with a bit more accuracy than Charlie, we can enjoy some success in the markets.

Over the years I have been fortunate enough to spot just a few big picture events. Firstly I backed the rise, and then the big fall, in interest rates from the late 80s to early 90s. Then I jumped onto the share market in the mid 90s as economies recovered from recessions and inflation stayed benign. I moved into technology stocks at that time, very late in some respects, but still five years before the so-called tech boom. The profits I made sheltered me through the subsequent bust, which destroyed many 'Johnny-come-lately' tech investors who jumped in during 1999 and 2000. Over these periods, I've also been happy to be on the right side of some big shifts in the US dollar.

There have been far more that I've missed! I did not get too involved in emerging markets, such as Russia and Turkey in the last few years. Nor did I play in some big swings in commodity prices, or in the biotech boom, or in hosts of others. There has been a lot going on around the world, and a lot of money has been made. Many of the hedge funds, which are more inventive and aggressive than the average fund, have done very well on these types of big moves.

The strategy here is that if you want to make big money, try looking for a big idea.

And the next Big Thing is...?

What do I think is going to be the next Big Thing? It's a tough question. Of course it could be China. There, the size of the economy is set to overtake that of France and the UK in the near future. I find it ironic that China is 'communist' because it is probably the most capitalist country in the world, with fierce competition, and few labour restrictions such as minimum wages.

China's massive supply of cheap labour, massive demand for raw materials, and massive market for western goods and technology will continue to produce winners and losers around the globe. Australia and other large exporters of raw materials are obviously well placed, and consumers in the western world will benefit from cheap goods and this will help inflation in those countries to stay under control. On the other hand, under-educated people in the west will suffer, because their jobs will be most at risk (for our generation, it is more important than ever to make sure the kids get to university!).

China will mean a lot more rich people. Europe in particular, has already seen the effects of wealthy Russians and their big spending on property. That will be nothing compared to the eventual spending power of wealthy Chinese. This could have a dramatic effect on desirable places such as the South of France, and unique locations such as Venice. It could also push prices higher for things like gold and contemporary art.

A bizarre global economy

It is amazing that China, the world's biggest poor country, is a lender to the rest of the world, while the world's biggest rich country, the United States, is a borrower. Who could have predicted that? Indeed, who can explain it? Normally of course, you would expect China to borrow as it rapidly enters the modern world and builds infrastructure and production capacity. And you would expect the US to be saving some of it's massive annual wealth creation, rather than borrowing more than half a trillion dollars per year.

Having said that, I am not overly concerned about borrowing by the US. They of course have fantastic wealth to repay debt. It's better for a rich man to rack up credit card bills, than a poor man.

To me, it is the economy of continental Europe which is more worrying, with it's reluctance to embrace greater competitiveness and innovation. Could this mean that the European share market and the Euro eventually fall behind?

Emerging products

Although in the last few years there has been an enormous level of interest in China and other emerging markets, as an investor, I have always been more interested in what I call 'emerging products'. The process of invention, research, development, and commercialisation of highly sophisticated products is faster than ever. Because it takes place mostly in the West, for me there are a lot of benefits in focusing on emerging products rather than emerging markets, such as legal protection, culture, language and distance.

There are many exciting areas. Nano-technology is the science of very, very small particles. These can produce new materials, and even create different substances like fuel additives to make fuel more efficient. Life sciences deal with the human body. The breaking of the human genome at the same time as the emergence of massive computing power has opened a whole new branch of medical science which could lead to cures for cancer, asthma, Alzheimer's and other diseases. It is even not impossible that within 100 years, scientists could be able to stop the human body aging, and that we could be the last generation that doesn't 'live forever'.

So we're on the verge of a massive wave of discovery. All of these things have crossed my mind and I've tried to position myself for a number of them.

In this section I've covered a whole spectrum of big picture ideas and opportunities.

The beauty of many of them is that you often have plenty of time to get involved. As I've stressed, the market takes time to adjust to structural changes, and often you'll see price trends develop which you can then use as signals to invest. However, you need to be patient, these things don't bear fruit overnight.

5.2 Ignore obscure theories and observations

This is consistent with looking for the next Big Thing. In my experience, obscure theories and observations rarely have an impact on the markets and never a lasting impact. So I learnt early on not to be distracted by the small things when looking for the big things.

I was at a meeting when a trader was predicting the upturn of the US economy. He'd noticed on his weekend trip that there were fewer homeless people on the streets of New York. While we're all happy if there are fewer homeless people, his observation was hardly a reliable indicator and, as it turned out, he was wrong.

Other things like brokers' tips can be just as useless. Remember, they have no successful track record and are not responsible for managing funds. I have often found that they are simply caught up in the gossip of the markets.

Another thing to avoid worrying about is who's buying and selling. Often you hear that mutual funds are buying this or that, and naturally there's a temptation to follow their lead. Resist it. There are buyers and sellers, and the price is where it is.

An obscure theory did tempt me once. It was years ago. I had a position in the Japanese markets, and I heard about an expert on Japanese earthquakes predicting that there was going to be an earthquake in Tokyo the following day. Now that might sound ridiculous, but the guy apparently had a track record after he had earlier successfully predicted two small earth tremors. This time he was predicting a much larger one. I thought seriously about what to do with this information. I fretted and fretted, and as it was I did nothing, and of course there was no earthquake.

5.3 Only invest in the broad markets when they are in line with the prevailing economic environment

The search for a big picture idea will sometimes take you to a specific niche. It may be a certain new technology which you believe is going to be a world beater. In that case, you may want to buy stocks in that sector, and your decision will be largely immune from the broader goings on in the economy.

However, when investing in the broad markets by taking a spread of stocks, bonds or commodities, the performance is likely to be dictated by the economy as a whole. The two key economic variables, inflation and economic growth, will be critical. Even though these two variables are very closely watched throughout the world, their movements and their impact on the markets are often underestimated and last for longer than generally expected.

Long term opportunities when you invest with the prevailing environment

In the early 1970s, OPEC raised oil prices, causing high inflation and poor growth. This big picture event literally caused a whole decade of poor stock market performance. It was an example of a huge event having a long lasting impact. In a completely efficient market, the price adjustment would have been a fast and massive drop in the market. Because the decline was slow and drawn out, you had some time to react and save yourself money.

In the late 80s and 90s the story was falling inflation caused by a host of fundamentals: competition, globalisation, technology, flexible labour rules, union co-operation, and the privatisation of government businesses. These things are very difficult to model and quantify, and many people underestimated them. They too caused a long drawn out result, which was a bull market in stocks and bonds.

You can see from these experiences that there are long term opportunities if you invest with the prevailing environment. The markets can be just as slow to react to inflation and growth as they are to other big picture influences. In the mid 1990s for example, I became convinced the economy was on the way up, and I had a fantastic ride in the stock market for nearly five years.

Be aware of the general economic situation

There are two ways to be aware of the general economic situation.

The easiest is to monitor the consensus view by staying in touch with the broad economic news and opinions. We will see in Strategy 9.5 that, far from being sceptical of the consensus view, I believe it is a very powerful and persistent driver of the market. Knowing the general state of the economy will steer you towards the right investment areas, if you follow the Strategies later in this chapter. Economic cycles often take years to complete, and there can be plenty of opportunities to jump on board.

The other way to monitor the economy is to analyse it yourself, and for that I recommend that you use the checklist in the following Strategy. Having more than a general idea of the economic conditions in this way allows me to react fairly quickly to economic cycles, which can be useful since the best trades may be when the economy is clearly starting to improve or deteriorate.

A final point is that being aware of the economic conditions can also be useful for defensive reasons. Even great ideas can struggle in bear markets, and it may be worth holding back until the economy is more favourable.

5.4 Be methodical – use a checklist to quantify and add rigour to a view

A view on the markets is a judgement about a number of fundamentals. For example, I will argue later that an investment in a small company usually involves a view on things like management, valuation, comparative advantage and product adoption.

It is very useful for any trade or investment to use the discipline of a checklist, where you list the fundamentals that you think are relevant and give them some kind of score. I would recommend that each fundamental be given a score between -3 and +3.

Benefits of a checklist

There are a number of benefits to the checklist procedure. Firstly, it forces you to consider a whole range of influences, and to not get carried away and ignore counter arguments. Secondly, the total score from the list is a measure of the strength of your view. Thirdly and finally, the checklist is a record of your view at a particular time which can be reviewed later to examine your trading technique.

As a big fan of checklists, I have used them to help evaluate many different markets. One colleague of mine went one step further. He rang me in Europe from Australia to discuss a checklist he was using to help decide whether to live in Sydney or Melbourne!

Here, I am going to explain how I developed a checklist for monitoring the economy. Don't worry if economic statistics are not your thing, you can skip the rest of this Strategy, as it is not fundamental to the 100 Strategies, or read on, since it is at least useful to know how the checklist functions. On the other hand, the benefits of closely monitoring the economy are that you can react more quickly when it changes.

I originally started using a checklist on the economy in my days at Bankers Trust. Back then, I loved working in a dealing room with masses of people. The camaraderie, friendships, exchange of ideas and goofing around was unbeatable. The people were intelligent, fun and quick witted. Really, the only part I didn't like was spending ages looking at screens and little numbers, and waiting for the release of economic statistics. The amount of data can be overwhelming and even the best traders can get lost in the detail.

Monitoring economic growth and inflation

Consequently, early in my career my team and I found that the best way to monitor the economic information was by a checklist. The list contained two sections, economic growth and inflation. These are the two key macroeconomic influences which feed into all the other statistics. A checklist may have looked similar to the one on the following page.

Checklist	
Economic Growth	
Retail sales	++
Employment	+
Housing	+
Consumer confidence	+
Business confidence	+
Industrial production	+
Government surplus/deficit	- -
Gross National Product	+
Total	6
Inflation	
Wages	- -
Unemployment	++
Exchange rate	+
Commodity prices	-
Input prices	-
Capacity utilisation	+
Total	0

In this example, growth looks good, while inflation is staying benign. You will see in the next Strategy that this would be a signal to head towards the share market.

Each score is given between -3 and +3, because trying to be more precise than that is spurious. We would generally look at things over a three-month time horizon, so if the current three months were better than the previous three months, we would give a positive score. In that way we avoided one-month blips and allowed time to see an economic trend develop. We could wait longer to be sure of a trend, but the trade off was that you could miss the boat if you waited too long.

The strength of the score was open to judgement, and we would have one eye on the consensus in the market place, so a fall in inflation would get a higher score if it was better than the market expected.

Individual members of the team were responsible for preparing the checklists for different countries, and they would present their results to the rest of us for debate. Suddenly these dry statistics burst into life! We would use the information to place positions in the market, so it was important to get it right, and sometimes the debate about the scores became very animated.

A check on getting carried away

When we were wrong, we had the checklists to look back on, and so could usually identify the source of our mistakes. We found that our judgements became better and better for the scores on the list. The other benefit of the checklists is that because they are designed to look broadly at all the information available, they force you to look at all sides of the argument. They can help stop you getting carried away.

Using this technique brought us a lot of success. For me it has been very useful in highlighting the turns in the economy over the past ten to fifteen years.

I am so confident of the checklist style approach that I have been doing some recent work on automating it to create a trading system. It will be a form of artificial intelligence and try to mimic the actions of a good trader. Then I can really relax and let the computer do all of the work!

5.5 Buy stocks when economic growth is strong and inflation is weak

The theme of this chapter is that markets are slow to react to structural changes. One major structural influence is the state of the economy, which can be monitored by keeping in touch with the consensus, or more closely by using a checklist. If an investor wants to use a view on the economy as an investment tool, they naturally need to know which assets are the most appropriate for different economic environments. This is the topic of this Strategy and the next three.

Timing is important

Here we look specifically at the broad stock market, such as the FTSE 100 or the S&P 500. My view on trading these markets is that, contrary to a lot of advice, we *should* try to get in and out at the right times, and that these markets *do* take time to react to the economy.

The following charts show the performance of the US stock market since 1900.

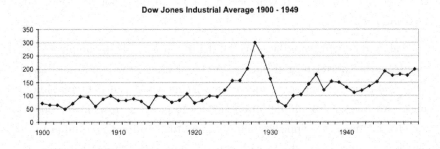

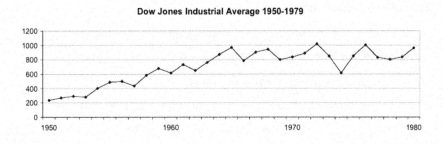

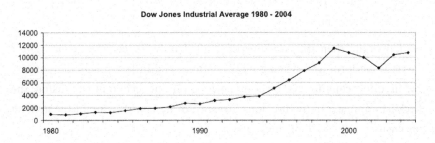

Source: Dow Jones, Wren Research

Stocks have moved in very broad cycles in the past hundred years or so. Roughly speaking, the 1920s, 1950s, 1980s and 1990s all saw long periods of favourable stock markets. The 1900s, 1910s, 1930s, and 1970s, as well as the early 2000s, were lousy.

I believe that these big moves are the ones that investors should focus on. It is worth trying to get them right. On the other hand, it is too ambitious to try to beat the general market by trading in and out more frequently. The stock market is the most analysed of all the markets, as you quickly realise if you compare coverage in the newspapers or on TV, to the amount given to the other markets.

To be able to benefit from these cycles, the investor needs to completely step back from the shorter-term influences on the markets. The important thing is to focus on the general environment and decide whether it is favourable for stocks. An investor should definitely not try to pick the turns in the market. The idea is almost the opposite: allow some broad consensus to build in the market and invest *after* the price begins to move. (This style of investing is key to these 100 Strategies and I will develop it further later on.)

Start with the economy

The starting point for looking at the big picture is probably the economy. Stocks do well with economic growth and low inflation, because:

1. Economic growth feeds into profits.
2. Low inflation allows lower interest rates, which benefit businesses.
3. Low rates increase the relative attractiveness of stocks as assets, and push prices higher.

(High inflation often leads to a high real interest rate, as central banks try to squeeze it out of the system, so there can be a double whammy pushing nominal interest rates higher.)

I would argue then that an investor should only expect the general stock market to perform well when growth is strong and inflation is under control. The investor can do his own homework on the economy by using the checklist approach in the previous Strategy, or by being aware of the general consensus on the state of the economy.

When looking at the economy, the investor obviously needs to be aware of what is going on in the world. Last century there were two world wars, a great depression, Vietnam and two oil crises. These events are obviously difficult to measure in economic terms, but they largely dominated the stock market much of the time, and contributed to the long periods of under or over- performance.

End of the cold war and the 1990s boom

One big event, which was positive for the markets, was the end of the cold war in 1989. That, combined with continued low inflation and a technology boom, helped the stock market to achieve a great performance in the 1990s. This was when I first put this Strategy into practice. I switched from bonds and started to invest in stocks in the early 1990s as I saw the economy climbing out of recession. Some commentators were actually worried about the possibility of inflation rising at that time, including Alan Greenspan who seemed worried about the rising gold price. That seemed odd to me, and I was proved right when interest rates stayed under control. The good run I had in the stock market lasted for over half a decade, and despite the nasty market tumble of 2000, my investments did very well overall.

Apart from looking at the economy and the big cycles, in the way I suggest, there has been an unbelievable amount of work done on trying to figure out what drives the stock market. The market has been analysed to the nth degree, and all sorts of theories and ideas have been examined.

There is plenty of data to analyse, and some analysts have looked back as far as the early 1800s. The interesting thing is that, to my knowledge, there has not been a lot discovered apart from a few broad theories.

Old theories may have had their day

One theory, which was popular a few years ago, is that investors should buy and hold their stock investments. They should not try to outguess the stock market. This idea became a mantra after the market recovered so well following the 1987 share market crash. The crash now only looks like a hiccough from the great bull market of the 1980s and 1990s. That recovery was a manifestation of the market's long term resilience.

A related theory is that the stock market should always outperform bond yields over the long run, as stock investors are compensated for the extra volatility.

These types of theories may have faded a little now, after global investors experienced a five year bear market that started in 2000. In the US, the broad stock market indices closed lower in 2005 than five years earlier. Five years is a long time, even for patient investors. I would also argue that as the buy and hold theories have become widely held, the effect has been to push prices higher, increasing the entry cost for new buyers and removing their attraction – a kind of self-defeating prophecy.

Other theories, based on ratios, such as price earnings ratios, would have been very effective in signalling the tech crash a few years ago. However, I think many of them would have been over cautious, and missed much of the fantastic bull market in the five years earlier. That would have cost investors a large amount of missed profits.

In summary, my advice is to choose the best periods to be invested in the share market. There are long periods of over and underperformance. Watch the economy and the big picture influences. I will explain later that the best way to time investments is to allow some broad consensus to build in the market and invest after the price begins to move.

5.6 Buy bonds when inflation and economic growth are both weak

Bonds are all about interest rates. Because they pay a fixed rate of return, their value goes up when market interest rates fall. People will pay more than $100 for a $100 bond, if it is paying 5% when market rates are only 4%.

Inflation has the bigger influence on bond yields

Ten year bonds tend to be the benchmark bond for most countries. Loosely speaking, in determining ten year rates the market takes a view of how short term rates, such as overnight or quarterly rates, will average out over the next ten years. This involves a view on inflation and economic growth. Historically, inflation has been the bigger cause of movements in bond yields and inflation has generally been more volatile with longer cycles than growth.

Bond market yields can be a useful indicator of the market's confidence in the authorities' ability to control inflation.

The big trends in the 20th century

The chart below shows the performance of US long term interest rates since 1950.

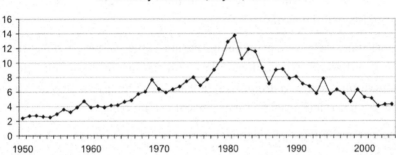

US Treasury Bond Yield, 10yrs+, 1950 - 2004

Source: US Federal Reserve Board

In the early 1950s, US bond rates were about 3%, not far off the 4% level today. During that time, they had two giant moves: a fairly steady rise over three decades to about 14% in 1981, and a fairly steady fall back in the following two decades.

Interestingly, bond yields had remained fairly steady in the first half of the 20th century as the bond market remained confident in the authorities' ability to control inflation. This was despite the big fluctuations caused by two world wars.

The rise in interest rates in the 1950s, 60s and 70s was due to a loss of that confidence. Most of the damage was done by the big oil price increases in the 1970s. What a miserable decade that was. The authorities' sharp increases in short term rates in the early 1980s started the turnaround of inflation, and consumers and the markets gradually lowered their inflation expectations.

These big moves in the bond markets offer long term trading and investment opportunities. By focusing on growth and inflation there can be plenty of time to place positions.

One of the greatest trends – the fall in bond yields from the late 1980s

My own experience trading in the bond markets started in the late 1980s. I had just set up a new strategic trading department at Bankers Trust. At that time we did well by getting on to a mini-trend of rising yields, which was a temporary reversal of the longer term trend of falling yields after 1980.

Within a couple of years we turned bullish as economic growth and inflation started to weaken. Our checklists on the economy were great at spotting the changing environment, and we were in line with a growing consensus by economists and the media.

At that time, there were many things pushing inflation lower: globalisation, falling inflation expectations, de-unionisation, privatisation, greater competition, more entrepreneurialism, technology and increasing productivity, Thatcherism and independent central banks.

I couldn't really think of anything pushing it the other way.

I love these trades, where all the fundamentals are either bullish or bearish. I find that **in these situations, markets can really move a long way, even after the view becomes quite mainstream.** There is also usually plenty of time to get on board, as the moves can take years to complete.

You will see later that I prefer having such a consensus on my side, rather than trying to be contrarian.

This is still one of the best macroeconomic opportunities that I have witnessed. I stayed on this trade in one way or another for nearly ten years. I was briefly shaken off my position in 1994 when economic growth picked up and bond rates rose from 6% to 8%. However, I jumped back on in 1995 for a 3% fall in yields over two or three years.

Along the way, I saw many traders stuck with the status quo. They could not believe that rates could simply keep falling. In Australia, I won a lot of friendly bets when rates broke through 10%; now they're about 5%.

I have not really been involved in the bond market since the late 1990s. There is not much going on now with bond yields, and over the last few years US ten year yields have been stuck between 3% and 5%. However, keep an eye on long term changes in economic growth, and especially on inflation. Things may change.

5.7 Buy commodities when inflation and economic growth are both strong

Commodities are raw materials. Economic growth is good for commodity prices because a growing economy needs more inputs. Inflation is also good for commodity prices because commodities are tangible assets rising in price as the value of paper money declines.

Like all markets, the commodity markets have some large moves driven by a consensus on the fundamentals, which drive the price further than generally expected. These are the type of moves that these strategies seek to identify and exploit. So the idea here is to identify those periods where growth and inflation are strong, and then to take a long term view with a trading position. These smooth changes are the sort of things that we are trying to identify.

Trade in a basket of commodities

To implement this Strategy, you will probably need to trade a basket of several commodities, rather than any specific item. This is because to get the net effect of growth and inflation, you will need to remove a lot of the randomness in the price caused by supply factors. I have discussed in Strategy 4.7 how these supply driven markets can present extra difficulties. These markets are often more turbulent. They can be influenced by events in remote countries, many of which can be unstable and corrupt. They can also be influenced by the random effects of the weather. You don't want your view that higher inflation will cause higher commodity prices to be upset by good weather causing a bumper crop in bananas.

Much of the information driving commodities can be quite obscure. It is a difficult task for investors to somehow get hold of that information. So by trading a basket of commodities, we will win some and lose some on the individual items, and allow the economic fundamentals to dominate. I'd rather do that than bet on whether there will be a bad season in an unpronounceable country.

CRB Index

While you can choose your own selection of commodities, it is probably easier to use an existing index. The most watched indicator index is known as the CRB Index. Futures and options on the CRB Index are traded on the New York Board of Trade. It is made up of different categories of commodities:

- **Energy**: crude oil, heating oil, natural gas
- **Grains**: corn, soybeans, wheat
- **Industrials**: cotton, copper
- **Livestock**: cattle, hogs
- **Precious metals**: gold, platinum, silver
- **Softs**: cocoa, coffee, orange juice, sugar

Because it covers such a diverse range of materials, its movements will mask moves in the individual components, and smooth out the supply problems I have mentioned. Obviously, there are many other commodities which are not included in the CRB Index.

As an alternative to trading an index on an exchange, there are a number of different ways to trade commodities - apart from keeping silos full of corn in your backyard. You can also invest in companies, such as steel companies or oil companies, which you feel will benefit from higher prices of their products. Or you can even go a step bigger, and buy into the currencies of countries which have a lot of natural resources.

Long periods of high growth and high inflation are rare

Any of these techniques could be used to implement this Strategy and follow a consensus on growth and inflation. In practice, though, there have not been many periods where growth and inflation are able to rise at the same time. Authorities normally respond to higher inflation by raising interest rates. They only have difficulty keeping a lid on inflation if raising rates weakens the economy too much. When there is strong growth, the authorities have a lot of room to move without causing a recession, and so they are able to stamp down on the inflation if necessary. Therefore, it has been rare to find long periods of high growth and high inflation.

This helps to explain why commodities have seen a 50 year or so price decline in real terms.

The following chart shows the performance of the CRB Index since 1950.

CRB Commodity Index 1950 - 2004

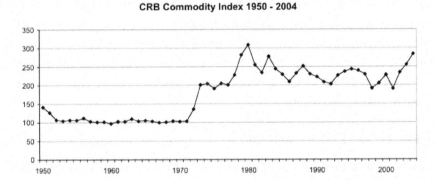

Source: Global Financial Data

In the 1970s, there was high inflation, largely caused by OPEC, without strong economic growth. Commodities had their best run for a long time but prices still barely rose in real terms, because inflation caused a tripling of average price levels.

The 1980s and 1990s saw the opposite experience, with falling inflation and many periods of good growth. This was miserable for commodity prices in real terms. The economic growth was not enough. The increased demand by the growing world economy was generally offset by falls in the costs of production and extraction due to dramatic improvements in technology. Technology also helped economies reduce their dependence on the more expensive commodities, such as oil. Social change also reduced the growth in demand for commodities, as economies became more service oriented, and less reliant on manufacturing.

The recent story has been all about China

Having said all of this, a new period has emerged over the last few years. Growing economies, particularly China, have experienced strong growth and inflation simultaneously. They have tolerated inflation, and let growth rage on. Commodities have had a renaissance. There has been debate about whether China will try to cool inflation, but in the meantime, commodity prices have soared as the hungry dragon searches the world for raw materials.

On the back of this, I bought Australian dollars in 2003 as a kind of commodity play. I agreed with the widespread view that Chinese demand for commodities would drive prices higher, and that Australia was well placed to benefit as a supplier. There were other things in favour of the Aussie dollar, such as strong growth and relatively high interest rates, which gave me added confidence. The trade has done well, and I still have it as I write. Given their lacklustre environment during most of my career, this is the closest I have come to trading in commodities.

Watch out for US dollar exposure

One word of warning on commodities. Since they are usually priced in US dollars, price moves can sometimes have more to do with dollar strength or weakness than with commodities. In periods of dollar weakness, for example, commodity prices may rise just to keep their European and Japanese price relatively stable. This is always an important consideration if you do not want to accidentally speculate on currencies.

5.8 Few assets benefit when inflation is strong and economic growth is weak

A combination of inflation and slow growth rarely helps any asset class. We had almost a decade of this in the 1970s, and stocks and bonds suffered miserably. Even commodities struggled to rise in real terms.

1970s – a miserable decade

You may remember the era. I moved into my teens and it was not a great decade to be growing up. Everyone seemed so miserable. OPEC hit the world with two oil price increases. In 1973, the price per barrel went from a few dollars to over ten dollars, and in 1979 from the low teens to over 30 dollars. The west was far more dependent on oil than today. It was like two punches in the stomach.

The oil price fed into just about all prices, and inflation went out of control. By 1980, it was around 10%. People were accustomed to cycles in the economy. Normally, inflation would only rise when the economy was doing nicely and it was the excess demand that pushed up prices. However, in the 70s, jobs were scarce as unemployment also headed towards 10%, and so there was plenty of unused capacity in the economy. This was inflation plus stagnation, and they had a nice word for it: *stagflation.*

I remember at school in the 1970s learning economics, and the subject of stagflation. No one knew what to do about it. I think in Australia they tried wage freezes. Unions were more powerful then, and tried to ensure their members' wages were maintained. In the UK, they had 'the winter of discontent' and things became so bad that they were ready for the dose of medicine called Thatcherism.

No easy answer to stagflation

However, what could the authorities have done? A rise in the price of oil is like a tax on the entire country. Just about everyone is going to be worse off, and there were bound to be fierce struggles over how the bill was divided. (The real tragedy of the time was the social effect that led to punk rock!)

Unfortunately, there is no easy policy the authorities can adopt to fight stagflation. The 'dismal science', economic theory, has done a lot for economic management in normal conditions. The greatest economist ever, John Maynard Keynes, told us what to do: increase and decrease the government budget to smooth out the economic cycles. When people are not spending, governments should do the spending for them, and borrow the money. How insane were governments to reduce, rather than increase, government spending in the Great Depression! On the other hand, if people are spending too much and the economy is overheating, governments should cut back.

Keynes did not really trust interest rates as an economic tool. One reason was that in a recession, an interest rate cut may not be enough to encourage overly pessimistic consumers and businesses to borrow and spend. You can only lead a horse to water. But again, in normal conditions, interest rates can be used very effectively. When inflation rises, a little tightening up of interest rates slows things down a little, and the inflation eases off. This method of controlling the economy has become even more important as politicians have hijacked the fiscal budget for politics, rather than economics.

The trouble with stagflation is that the authorities don't know whether to boost the economy or to slow it down. Trying to create jobs risks even higher inflation, and trying to solve the inflation problem makes the job situation even worse. So it is not clear what to do with the budget balance or with interest rates.

These problems for the economy and the policy makers are reflected in the markets, and there is nothing attractive to investors. All you can do is to stay in cash, and to sell the other markets.

The stagflation of the 1970s only really ended when the US Federal Reserve gave the economy a sharp dose of very high interest rates in the early 1980s, and allowed a recession. Hopefully we will not get another decade like the 70s for a long time.

5.9 You are unlikely to out-analyse the analysts

The ideas I have discussed in this chapter relate to opportunities in the markets, which arise from the markets taking too long to adjust to big picture changes in the economy and society. By identifying and understanding these big picture changes, I believe we can take on the biggest markets in the world and win. Most of these big changes are extremely hard to quantify and everyone is in the same situation.

Detailed analysis is not much use, because the task is really about keeping up with, and thinking about, the broader issues and their repercussions, rather than number crunching or looking for more detail.

I love big picture investing. It is extremely interesting because it relates to such fundamental factors in our lives and any research doesn't get overly specific, nor involve mind-numbing detail. I have discussed some examples of big picture ideas, such as big drops in inflation, the rise and tumble of the technology sector and the rise of China. If you can make some attempt to understand these things, you can make a lot of money.

Top-down over bottom-up

When you move away from big picture influences, you start looking at specifics. You might look at IBM for example, and try to decide if it is a buy or sell. This requires more detailed analysis. We move from a 'top-down' to a 'bottom-up' approach. Here you lose the comparative advantage of the market's uncertain response to the big picture, and you rely on your analysis being better than other peoples'.

This is a tough call. Do you really think you could spot a mistake in the market's valuation of IBM? I couldn't. I would only trade the stock on the basis of a big picture view, which would probably lead me to take a position in the share index or a sector index as a whole. I think it is a mistake to try to out-analyse the analysts. I know of traders who get research notes and do a lot of homework on some of these big companies, and I strongly believe they are wasting their time. The traders' results are usually caused by movements in the general market or by luck, rather than by superior analysis of a specific stock.

Fortunately, not all markets are as heavily analysed as IBM's. This is where I believe you need to choose smaller, less analysed markets if you want an edge. You could examine some of the smaller currencies, interest rates and property markets. However, what interests most people is the share market. In the next chapter, I will discuss small stocks, and why I prefer them to the bigger ones. Leave IBM for the next guy.

6 | Small Companies

6.0 Small companies offer more opportunities than large companies

This chapter is specifically about opportunities in the share market. Naturally there is a lot of media attention given to the blue chip stocks and to other large companies. With this amount of attention, I firmly believe that it is the smaller companies that have a greater chance of being wrongly priced.

That is not to say that all small companies are good value. There are probably as many that are overvalued, as are undervalued. However, some investigation and analysis may help you distinguish the small companies that are undervalued.

My experience with small companies has mostly been with unlisted private companies (private equity), and with listed stocks on the Alternative Investment Market (AIM) in London. Not everyone can invest in private equity, because it normally involves having contacts to make the introductions, and because sometimes the minimum investment size is too large for many investors. Listed markets like AIM and NASDAQ, however, are more accessible for all investors, so this may be where you want to look.

What is a small company?

My idea of a 'small' company is something valued at less than US$250 million – in practice, my preference is to look at companies of less than US$100 million. I firmly believe that it is easier for these small companies to double in value, than it is for larger companies. Of course, there is also the higher risk of failure, but that is where skill plays a role in choosing the right investments. The small companies have the advantage that they are often too small to attract the attention of big investment funds, and consequently they can be wrongly priced.

This chapter will not be a treatise on stocks. The strategies here reflect my own approach to investing in small companies. There has been an enormous amount written on stocks, and I would not pretend to be an expert on all the different theories and history. Like all of my trading, my ideas are home-grown and I endeavour to do things for logical reasons.

I had no experience investing in stocks until the mid 1990s. At that time, the western economies were recovering from recession and were starting to grow, without any worrying increases in inflation. Using the investment ideas outlined in chapter 5, I thought, "Okay, time to invest in the share market". I was also looking for the next Big Thing, and so I chose to focus on the technology sector. It was a good choice: for the next six years or so, technology stocks went crazy. This great run gave me a strong buffer against the tech wreck that followed.

Small companies offer the best risk-reward ratio

What interested me most were small companies. It was my view that despite their high failure rate they offered the best risk-reward, particularly if diversification could be used to reduce the average risk. In putting this theory into practice, it made sense for me to start with unlisted companies. Normally the companies had a market value of between half a million and two million pounds. These young companies were often too early in their growth to have profits or even sales.

Since then, I have invested in many unlisted companies, and have been nominated as one of the top ten business angels in Europe. Although technology has been an ongoing theme, I have backed all sorts of other companies as well, including a diamond mine in Sierra Leone, a private members' club, a sporting goods retailer and a corporate advisory business.

Usually I have invested in an existing business which needs more money to expand or continue. At other times, I have backed the creation of a completely new business, sometimes in partnership with Oxford University and one of their professors.

Small companies have a high failure rate

Naturally, to continue doing this you need to have ways to extract your profits if the company succeeds. Normally this would be by the company listing on the share market, or by it being acquired by another company. On the other hand, these new companies have a high failure rate, and often you simply lose all of your investment. Of the 52 companies I have backed:

- 3 have been sold to bigger companies;
- 13 have listed on the share market;
- 10 are still private but progressing;
- 10 are still private and not doing too well; and
- 16 have gone bust.

So all in all, 26 wins and 26 losses. This is considered a very good ratio in the venture capital business.

It was challenging in the early days to learn about a new investment sector, and I made many mistakes. I would say I invested in about twenty companies before I really had a clue. Fortunately, the strong share market at the time saved me from a few disasters, as there was always plenty of investor demand to support companies that otherwise would have failed.

Small listed companies can be similar to unlisted companies

Over time, I also started to invest in small listed companies, particularly on the AIM market in London. I had noticed that because of their small size, they were also prone to being wrongly priced by the market. They also continued to face many of the challenges faced by the unlisted companies.

How to start

There are thousands of small companies listed on the market. Some of these may offer special opportunities, but how does an investor filter out the uninteresting ones, and derive a manageably small list of companies to consider? I would suggest that it is best to focus on:

1. Companies involved in activities where you have some particular expertise, involvement or interest. If your hobby is boating, for example, you could come across a company making a new, more efficient propeller, and make an investment.

2. Companies which fit your big picture view. If you expected nanotechnology to take off, you could seek out available investments in that area.

3. Companies that are referred to you by people whose opinion you respect.

Once you find an investment that appeals to you, it is quite straightforward if the company is listed, since you can buy shares on the market through a stockbroker.

Investing in unlisted companies

Unlisted companies are not listed on any stock market, so buying shares is not simple. It is usually necessary to make contact with the company directly, and then to participate in their next round of fundraising.

An easy way to start investing in unlisted companies is to join a private investor network, which are semi-formal groups of investors who have relationships with unlisted companies. These investors meet regularly to discuss ideas and present investment opportunities they have come across. For example, a member may hear of a small company which needs to raise one million pounds. The investor may only want to invest, say, 50 thousand himself, and so they bring the idea to the other members to help raise the balance. It is then up to these other members to decide as individuals, whether they invest and for what amount. Some of these investor groups also produce newsletters and websites covering their activities. One such group in the UK that I have had contact with is The Great Eastern Investment Forum (www.geif.co.uk) which is based in Cambridge.

More risky

Small companies, listed and unlisted, are generally riskier than the broad markets. As I have emphasised, they are often young and unproven, with some chance of either fantastic success or complete failure. Therefore, it is essential that investors follow the risk guidelines I have outlined earlier in the book. In particular, investors should start with small-sized investments and try to diversify where possible.

The small company checklist

> Of the companies that I consider, I probably only invest in one out of ten.

Investors in small companies should also be very discriminating. There is a huge variation in the quality of the potential investments. Of the companies that I consider, I probably only invest in one out of ten.

Over the years, I have become convinced that there are a number of criteria necessary for a company to succeed. These are listed below.

Checklist for small companies

1. Management
2. Valuation
3. Initial comparative advantage
4. Sustainability
5. Adoption of product
6. Ability to handle growth
7. Route to exit and cash resources*
8. Other shareholders*
9. Due diligence*

The final three are marked with an asterisk as they only apply to unlisted companies.

The checklist can be used in the way described in Strategy 5.4 where I recommended the use of checklists to monitor market fundamentals. That would involve giving each item a score ranging from -3 to +3, and deriving a total score. Alternatively, it can simply be used as a list to check if the company meets all the criteria. Either way, the idea is to adopt a disciplined approach to investing.

Each of the items are discussed one-by-one in the rest of this chapter.

6.1 The quality of a company's management is by far the most crucial factor in determining its success

I am convinced about this Strategy. I have seen bad management mess up the most amazing opportunities where companies have failed despite having everything else going for them.

With my early investments, I made many mistakes by focusing too much on the product, and not enough on the management. Now, I realise that good management will find a way to make their product work, while poor management can mess up good products.

Even big companies can make mistakes. Xerox had a fantastic product in photocopiers in the 1970s (the name was synonymous with the product: you 'Xeroxed' something). They had a fantastic platform to expand into the technology market, by developing printers and similar devices, yet a few years ago the company was struggling to survive. They've had a very tough time after never really grabbing the opportunity. It does seem to have been a management problem.

On the other hand, good management can often build something out of almost nothing. They are good at developing the business in the right direction. They spot opportunities, and have creative solutions. If their products are not selling, they may find ways to improve the product by research and development, or by buying or merging with other companies. They can weed out the wrong people and they face up to difficulties early.

It is easier to assess the management of smaller companies than larger ones.

There is a much greater variation in the level of talent within smaller companies. Just about all managers of big companies are very talented, even those who fail. Unfortunately, for smaller companies that is not always the case.

During the tech wreck, I saw many small tech companies fail while others somehow survived. The survivors generally had good management. They weren't necessarily those with the best product, but they were those that cut expenditure when times were getting tough, and made plans for keeping the business alive for three or four years until the market recovered.

Face to face meetings are important

To help determine the quality of the management there is nothing quite as useful as a face to face meeting. You find out a lot in the first five minutes. This instinct is so often correct that I have usually regretted the times when I have ignored it.

I once invested in a small listed company, but when I visited the CEO, I knew immediately that I had made a big mistake. The office of the guy was completely covered in papers, faxes and other junk - I'd never seen anything like it in all my life. I'm not joking, but you had to walk across the papers to get to his desk. It wasn't in piles or any order, it was just scattered everywhere. He obviously had no system, and when I saw that I thought, "This is a problem!". It obviously was a problem and the company soon failed, costing me over a million dollars. Yet when I had talked to him over the phone, he was a very convincing guy - it was only through meeting him that I found out the real story.

Here is another advantage of focussing on smaller companies - you have more chance of getting some of their time. Big companies will certainly squeeze very large fund managers into their diaries, but they may not be as willing to meet with smaller investors. A friend of mine in Australia does well by investing small amounts in small listed companies, and by making the effort to see their management in person. He is often amazed by the friendly and open reception.

The track record of the managers is also very useful.

Sometimes a manager is very appealing because previously they have taken a company all the way from nothing to a good valuation. They may have built up a good reputation and made money for themselves in the process, and you know that they have choices apart from working for the company in which you're potentially investing.

Management strategy can also reveal a lot about their quality. Watch what they're doing - Hewlett Packard merges with Canon, Microsoft moves into TV software etc. Many investors focus too much on current revenue and profits while ignoring strategy. It's this that can be vital to a company's future, particularly with smaller companies that have fewer resources to recover from mistakes.

6.2 Determining the fair valuation is more difficult with small companies

Naturally, you need to look at a company's valuation when you are considering investing. However, this is usually more difficult with smaller companies because they are often growing quite rapidly. You could use standard measures such as the price-earnings ratio as a guide, but the problem is of course, that you are less sure of the level of any future earnings.

My normal approach is to only invest if I think the valuation is ridiculously cheap. This approach requires patience, because I have to consider and reject many possibilities. Only with smaller companies would I find the sort of opportunities that I am after.

Any attempt at determining valuation involves a consideration of:

- the size of the potential market;
- the chances of winning some of that market; and
- the amount of money required.

But be careful. Many business plans are based on getting a tiny percentage of a huge market, but that's not as easy as it sounds. To be flippant, don't think that starting a chocolate factory is a good idea just because world chocolate sales are in the billions and you only need 0.00001% of the market to make a profit. The hardest part is often getting any sales at all.

Large share of a small market is preferable to small share of a large market

For this reason, I usually prefer businesses which are shooting for a large percentage of a smaller market. They are often trying to create a new market or to introduce 'disruptive technology' against the usual way of doing things. Usually they do not have much competition, and the company sinks or swims on its own merits.

Consequently, I often invest in completely new technology and concepts. I have backed things like new food scanning technology, drugs and cancer research, nanotechnology to reduce fuel consumption, broadband software for TV and a unique style of private members' club in London. All of these companies were looking to capture a big percentage of their market. Depending on their size at the time, these companies may or may not have had strong sales when I invested. If they did, it obviously gave me more confidence and I was happy to pay a higher share price.

Kangaroo valuation

To finish this section, here is a story which illustrates that many people do not have the vaguest notion of what companies are worth.

A good friend of mine in Australia had invested $100,000 of his money into a newly started business which planned to export kangaroo meat. It was a lot of money for him, and he came to me a little concerned that it was going wrong. The first thing I said to him was "mate, you know I've been doing a lot of this type of investing. You should have asked my opinion before you put money in". Anyway, I agreed to meet one of the managers, who was the guy who had approached my friend and persuaded him to invest.

The company was a complete start-up. There was just a handful of people involved, and I don't think they even had anyone full-time. They had no sales, and were putting efforts into trying to open up the US market. Apparently, kangaroo meat is the only type of meat which can actually lower cholesterol levels, rather than increase them. The plan was to get the interest of health conscious Americans. The company believed they had a comparative advantage because they had the use of a technology to make the meat easier to prepare. Kangaroo meat can be notoriously tough, but by selling it precooked, the consumer only needed to boil it in a special wrapping, and it would be nice and tender.

I had a few problems with the business model. Why was a tiny business trying to open a completely new market on the other side of the world? My instinct would have been to start on local territory in Australia, where surely there are also enough health conscious people who want to lower their cholesterol. However, my main concern was the way the business was funded. It seemed to be just by my mate's one hundred grand, which had run out. Now they wanted him to give them some more. As I raised this issue, the meeting turned a bit frosty. I had tried to establish from my mate what percentage of the company he had received for his investment, and he had no idea. So now I was asking the manager. I was shocked at the answer: "He's getting ten per cent."

If you put one hundred thousand into a business and receive ten per cent of the shares, this puts a valuation of the business at one million. There is no way you could value this business anywhere near that. The manager didn't agree. This business could be worth zillions, he said.

It got worse. The manager had given himself thirty per cent of the shares. His justification was that the business was his concept, and that he received no salary. I pointed out that three hundred thousand dollars was a lot for an unproven idea and a part-time commitment.

"I haven't made three hundred grand on this."

"But my mate has paid one hundred grand for a third of the shares you have. So yours must be worth three hundred. That's if he hasn't paid too much."

"That's if you want to believe that 'text book' stuff. We operate in the *real* world here."

The business went nowhere. It would have taken a miracle for my mate to make any money at that valuation. Happily, kangaroos are still safe from millions of hungry Americans.

6.3 Clearly identify the comparative advantages

As I like to invest in companies that can capture a big share of their market, I usually need to look for something different in a business, and to identify a killer application. I am rarely interested in 'me-too' businesses which are up against a lot of competition.

The saddest day of my business career was the day we sold our private members' club, Home House. We had received an offer that was simply too good to refuse, even though it did not result in a huge percentage return. Besides being a very different sort of investment for me, the club had proved to be a lot of fun over the years. I was sad to see it go.

There was some satisfaction however, because we could be proud of what we had created. We had used our comparative advantages to create a big success.

Eight years earlier, Brian Clivaz had presented to me his concept of a private members' club in London. He showed me a magnificent Georgian building, which was built by the famous architect Robert Adam for the Countess of Home in the 1770s. It had been empty for twelve years, simply because no one knew what to do with it. In its history, it had been home to all sorts of interesting people, such as Earl Grey, of the tea fame, and Anthony Blunt, of the spying game. It had also served as the French Embassy during the revolution. With its amazing staircase and ornate rooms, it was absolutely stunning and I fell in love with it.

Brian's idea was to create a club with fantastic drawing rooms, a health spa, eighteen hotel rooms, a restaurant, a bar and a courtyard. I liked the concept, and I had a few ideas of my own.

I want women

When I visited London from Monaco, I stayed in nice hotels, but often they were incredibly stuffy. To go to the bar for a drink, you were required, without exception, to wear a tie. (They'd kindly help out by lending a polyester yellow one.) The contrast with, say, New York, was striking. Bars there were full of smart, fun people, who were casually dressed. So I insisted to Brian that the club have no dress code. Mobile phones should also be permitted. I also had another condition: lots of women members! One business plan I could never understand was members' clubs with no women. This rather bizarre, very British thing, is weird. I knew that if the girls would come to the club, so would the guys.

Not a popular idea at first

I asked a few people what they thought of the idea. Most were against it. One view was that the club's joining fee and yearly fee were too expensive at £1,500 each: "It will be viewed as elitist."

Some didn't like the location. "It would be on the wrong side of Oxford Street", one Londoner told me, since the building was just outside the Mayfair area. I thought, "Near enough is good enough". I had always wondered, jokingly, why London's streets are named after the Monopoly board. We would be pretty close to its best property.

An expensive and difficult project

Despite the negativity, I decided to back the idea and I was the largest investor and later chairman. It was an expensive and difficult project. The building needed extensive restoration and decoration, which took nearly two years, and the cost quoted in the press of £12 million was only a mild exaggeration. I remember thinking, "well, if it doesn't work as a business, at least we've restored an important English masterpiece - not bad for an Aussie!". The problems and delays were the subject of a BBC documentary, 'Trouble At The Top'. It featured Brian's struggle to get the work finished and the club open on time. I was portrayed as the worried money guy from Monaco, but the delays were not really a concern to me. For me, the success of the business would depend on enough people eventually joining, even if that happened six months later than planned.

Eventually, we got the thing going and it was a great success. It became the celebrity club of London and attracted over 2,500 paying members. Each week there seemed to be another famous face. Names like: Brad Pitt, Robert Redford, Madonna, Sting, Will Smith, Elton John, Mick Jagger, and almost Bill Clinton, who apparently had to be refused entry because he came after closing time. I had one of the most memorable moments when Paul McCartney's first words to me were "I know you". He had seen the BBC documentary and decided to have a party at Home House, to follow his memorial concert for Linda at the Royal Albert Hall.

The importance of a comparative advantage

We had taken a big risk with Home House. We spent a lot of money, and it could easily have gone wrong in many ways. What always gave me confidence, though, was that we had a comparative advantage. There was a gap in the choice of places to wine and dine in London. We invented a genre. Nowhere else offered the combination of a historic and beautiful building with a casual atmosphere. Foreigners loved the Englishness, and the English loved the foreigners. At first, there were many issues with the service, since it was not easy opening a business with over one hundred employees. But even that quirkiness seemed to add a charm to the place.

Apart from creating a new genre, we had another advantage. The structure of a club with membership fees was better than just opening to the public and charging high prices to meet our costs. This was not a new concept, but still a great idea if it could be done. Once we had thousands of members, we had terrific membership income. This income stream meant that every day we opened with a profit, and we could give some of it back to members, by charging very reasonable food and beverage prices. Later, when I invested in a restaurant, I saw the stark reality of opening every day with a loss, and hoping that enough customers would arrive to push us into profit.

Delays: Viability or timing?

As I mentioned, Home House had been under pressure to open on schedule. While some of the investors were worried about a delay, I was not overly concerned, because a delay had no bearing on the long term viability of the business. If it was a good idea, it would still be a good idea six months later.

I have often seen investors being spooked by delays. On the share market, an announcement of a delay in say, a product launch, often results in a sharp sell-off. I believe that this price behaviour is an inefficiency, and that markets can over-react to timing issues, particularly for smaller companies.

It is a good strategy to watch for buying opportunities when prices fall on these announcements. When you believe that a company is still viable and maintains its comparative advantage, there may be a good chance of a healthy bounce.

6.4 Be sure the business is sustainable

Questions that I ask myself before investing in a business include:

- How sustainable is the business? It may have a comparative advantage, but will it last?
- What changes in the market place could destroy or add to the advantage?
- How will competitors react to the business?
- What room for error does the company have?

One of the most exciting companies I have ever come across is IP2IPO, which is listed on the London AIM market. It *has* to be the perfect example of a sustainable company.

IP2IPO is run by a very good mate of mine, David Norwood. He is a chess grandmaster who I met in the mid 1990s when he came to Bermuda to play chess. I liked him immediately and we quickly became friends. He's from northern England with a very sharp mind and a quick wit.

Wild pigs and volleyball

David and I have had a lot of fun over the years. We've cruised around London aimlessly, drinking champagne in a limo with Anatoly Karpov (a Russian and former world chess champion), and any girls we could find. We've shot wild pigs (and almost ourselves) in the top end of Australia, been chased by snakes in Thailand, crossed dangerous rivers in Africa in dodgy canoes, and played volleyball on the beach in Mahabalipurum, India, with hundreds of local kids.

Along with that, we've talked a lot about business. Dave is an Oxford graduate in history and joined Bankers Trust in London in the early 90s. He was hired as part of an idea to recruit chess players, with the reasoning that they would do well in finance. The logic stopped there however, because they gave him the most meaningless job and shouted at him. In my opinion intelligent people do worse than average at menial tasks. Anyway, it introduced him to the business world, and by the time we met, he was working for a small private bank and investing clients' money in small companies. It was Dave who piqued my interest in these opportunities, and in the late 90s, we started to explore his contacts with Oxford University. I eventually invested in a number of spinout companies from the University. We financed some promising research and tried to commercialise it. It was a new experience for the University and ourselves, but we learnt a lot along the way.

In 2000, Dave set up a business to advise small companies called IndexIT, with me as a backer. We eventually sold this to an investment house, and Dave set up IP2IPO under their ownership.

IP2IPO is really an extension of what we were doing with the universities, though now I am only a small shareholder. Dave has made the spinout process an art form - if he ever writes *his* 100 Strategies, you should sell this book and buy that one. What he has done with IP2IPO is to buy the right to commercialise research from Oxford and other universities by creating spinout companies. IP2IPO has either paid up front or committed to minimum investments for these exclusive rights. The idea is to eventually list these new companies on the share market, and IP2IPO can then choose to sell its stake. To date it has achieved a number of listings, and it has a large cash balance from earlier fund raisings.

Immune to the economic cycle and investment fashions

Now the amazing things about IP2IPO are that it is largely immune to the economic cycle or investment fashions, and that it really has no competitors. It can sit back while a whole lot of research goes on in the universities and then pick and choose the likely winners to spinout. It then provides a service by finding good managers for the new businesses, and by helping raise further funds if they are needed for the infant company. The whole process is good for society as worthwhile projects like cancer research are commercialised.

I have been telling my friends that IP2IPO is a good investment since it listed late in 2003. In just over a year, the share price more than doubled, while the general market was lacklustre. Since then it has pulled back by about a third. The market capitalisation is currently about £230 million, and I think they have about £100 million in cash. How could you value this company? I don't know, but I feel if one or two of their spinouts go really well, it could go crazy.

I believe that most companies would have trouble matching IP2IPO's sustainability. It is a good example of what you should look for. When looking at a company from the point of view of sustainability, look at factors like the ability to diversify the product and to reinvent the business if needed. Look out for the possible competitive behaviour, particularly if a bigger company may want to destroy the business. Keep in mind the 'barriers to entry' - the protection from competition - such as patents, inventions and lead times in development.

6.5 Good products don't always sell

There is a host of reasons for good products not selling: price, image, reliability, servicing, loyalty to competing products, company relationships, bad mouthing by competitors, politics within a buyer's organisation (careers tied to an alternative product) and nervousness that the selling company is too small or unreliable. I had my own lesson in marketing when I found that it was hard to sell a good quality product at a fraction of the normal price.

My dotcom flirtation

I started MegaAge.com in the middle of the dotcom boom. It was my only flirtation with the dotcom sector. It was an experiment really: I wanted to see if I could develop a brand name. So I started selling tennis racquets on the web, at cost price. My friends thought I'd gone crazy, and maybe they were right. But I thought that the racquets would sell like hot cakes, and the benefit would be that the brand, MegaAge.com, would become well-known, and then I could take it further.

Since moving to Monaco in the mid 90s, I've played a lot of tennis. It's fantastic having the Monte Carlo Country Club just down the road. There are 23 beautiful clay courts, and you can see the mountains on one side and the sea on the other. You don't make a reservation, but you always get a court. By comparison, when I'm in London, it's a nightmare to try to play - fight the traffic each way and get a court for just an hour. Living in Monaco has spurred my interest in tennis. I have found it a good way to keep fit, and much more interesting than the gym. Despite my serve, and my ground-strokes, I'm still an enthusiastic player!

Good quality at cost price

Talking to tennis players, I was amazed to find that even top quality tennis racquets, which are typically made in Asia, cost no more than $20 to make. They sell in the stores for over $200. Now I guess everybody has marvelled at retail mark-ups at one time or another, but I decided to do something about it. Since there is no patent on the basic tennis racquet design, I thought I'd make a whole bunch and sell them at cost. So I created MegaAge.com, and as a little side venture, put on soccer balls and basketballs as well. The products were very high quality, which didn't push up the cost price by much. I had two goals: to sell at low prices, and to compete with the best brand names out there. I'd met Pat Cash, the former Wimbledon champion, and Pat was more than happy to endorse the racquets. 'Pat Cash In Love' was one of the little adverts we ran in the English papers - referring to our racquets, of course.

The racquets sold well in the beginning. The adverts had an effect and we sold a few hundred in the first few months.

From that point, I was hoping that sales would really benefit from word of mouth. I knew that one challenge we needed to overcome was customer reluctance to buy unseen products from an unknown website. After enough people had bought racquets, I hoped that we would start to establish some credibility in the market place.

The problem was, though, when we didn't advertise, we didn't sell. Advertising is expensive, especially when you're trying to sell at cost. So we had to stop the adverts, and the company just ticked along on very low sales. The hoped for ramp-up in sales didn't happen.

A further problem was that we had a massive inventory of racquets. It really was silly. There was something like 10,000 racquets sitting in warehouses around the world, and we were selling handfuls. At a charity function at around that time, I won a prize in a raffle - two tennis racquets! I gave them back to be redrawn - I must have owned more racquets than anyone else on the planet.

In the end, I sold the stock and brand name for a fraction of the cost price. The buyers are friends of mine, who hopefully have the time and energy to make it a success. The idea may still be sound, if is combined with the right execution. So MegaAge.com lives on. After salaries, advertising and inventory costs, my three year flirtation with e-commerce cost me around half of a million dollars.

First, test the concept

It was an expensive lesson. Why did it fail? Clearly, not enough people knew about MegaAge. Marketing is not a waste of money for businesses. We should have allocated our resources better, by spending less on inventory and more on promotion. From a financial point of view, I should have tested the idea with a much smaller amount of money. For so many new businesses, the best idea is to *spend the minimum amount of money to test whether the basic idea is sound.* Why spend more than you must, to find out if you have a comparative advantage? It would have made more sense for MegaAge to make say, a thousand racquets rather than ten thousand. If the thousand had sold out, the business could then have ordered more.

The MegaAge racquet did seem to have an image problem with many people. Interestingly, the low price itself was sometimes a problem. Who likes to be seen with cheap equipment? In addition, people naturally assume there's something wrong with it, and are more critical than when they pay a higher price. Some feedback we received from buyers just did not make sense, given that the racquet was almost an exact copy of an expensive, branded model. Some coaches would bad-mouth the racquet. It seems some of them have side deals with the pro-shops, so it wasn't in their interests to promote our products.

Perhaps tennis players were not the best demographic group to offer an inexpensive product to in the first place. It is expensive to play tennis, with the court hire, tennis balls and coaching. If you can afford all of that, maybe you're not looking to save a few dollars on a racquet. It could have been better to focus on the soccer balls, where the buyers are not restricted to more affluent people.

So a compelling product is not always enough for a business to succeed. There are scores of examples in the corporate world of the best product not succeeding. While there is an element of randomness and luck, the execution is important, and again, that's up to the management.

6.6 Growth puts strains on small companies

Even with strong management and a compelling idea, it may not be easy for a small company to make the big-time. There can be all sorts of hurdles to overcome along the way, and each represents a real chance of failure.

Food scanning

One very exciting company, in which I am involved, is a world leader with its technology and has attracted some attention. Spectral Fusion Technologies is a Birmingham based company that sells machinery to food producers. The machines scan food by x-ray and analyse the results by computer. The main product has been a scanner for chicken fillets, which identifies and rejects those where it detects a bone. Historically, chicken food manufacturers have done this checking by hand. Before packaging, each fillet is picked up and examined while going along a conveyer belt. Bone Scan tries to offer a more reliable solution, which also reduces labour costs. The company's other products are in the fish, beef and pork industries, although these are in various stages of development.

Spectral was set up in the mid 1990s to use the expertise of one of the leading researchers in the world of scanning software. His knowledge was applicable in many different industries, such as screening baggage at airports, but he chose the food industry because the high volume and high-speed requirement offered him the best chance to add value.

Fishing for whales

Spectral is a small company that employs fewer than twenty people and tries to sell machines for hundreds of thousands of dollars. A good result would be selling one machine every one or two months. Obviously, each sale is a big deal, and the company sweats over every sales lead. They have described it as "fishing for whales", where you either win big or lose big.

To make sales, Spectral needs to convince buyers to adopt its products. I covered the problem of adoption in the previous Strategy. For technology companies this has extra challenges, because of the risks for buyers if the technology doesn't work or is not supported properly. For most Bone Scan buyers, x-ray represents a new way of dealing with bones. It is not a matter of them just upgrading an existing machine to something more modern and better.

Spectral has made a good effort at winning adoption. They have sold many machines to huge food suppliers. Some of the suppliers have been pushed by the big retailers to use Bone Scans. The retailers do not like any reports of bones found in fillets, and people have been known to choke on them.

It makes sense in today's world that bones are found by computer technology. Obviously, there are significant development costs, and Spectral is yet to turn a profit.

Problems of dealing with large companies

For a small company to make the breakthrough to revenue and profit growth, there are a host of other problems. Being a small company is not easy, especially when most of your dealings are with much larger companies. This can make sales negotiations very one-sided. The big boys know that they are very important to Spectral. It often seems that a firm sales agreement has been reached, but the buyer tries to 'chip away' at the deal, and get a better price or more features added. At times, there has been the opportunity to collaborate with large companies in the development of new products. Spectral has to be careful that the other companies are serious, and are not just trying to get a look at their technology to steal ideas. Of course, these types of things happen with all companies, big and small. However, for a smaller company, it is obvious to outsiders that for you, the stakes are high, and it's harder to play the poker game.

Resources are often stretched

Lack of resources is a big problem to small companies such as Spectral. There have been times when it has been necessary to pass up promising opportunities because of the cost and manpower required. Because the company has made losses, there has been a continual need for fundraisings. This takes up valuable management time and energy, in a company that is already very busy. Documents and shareholder updates have to be prepared, and presentations made to potential investors.

The challenge of international markets

Distance is another challenge for Spectral. There have been some sales in Europe, but the big market has been in the United States. Apart from the added difficulty in gaining credibility with the Americans because of the 'not invented here' syndrome, the distance creates another challenge for sales and servicing. There is a local agent on the ground in the US, but there is a continual need for Spectral to send people across the Atlantic. Sometimes this is to Alaska, where the company is developing applications in the fish industry. (They're quite good at finding fish bones, and now they're working on finding worms in the fish.)

Recently one executive tried to relocate his family to Atlanta, which was a disaster. It started badly with some baggage getting lost on the way, and got worse with a car accident due to the unfamiliarity of driving on the opposite side of the road. Meanwhile, the backyard of the house had some flooding. It was all too much, especially for the wife who was pregnant and looking after their two-year-old son. The relocation idea was abandoned and everyone came home.

Despite all of these difficulties, Spectral is making slow but sure progress towards profitability. They believe that x-ray and automation will be the way the food industry deals with bones, as it moves towards better food safety and lower labour costs. They plan to be the ones to provide the technology. As an investor, I need to assess the challenges they face, and weigh the risks against the potential rewards. I am sticking by them.

6.7 Be sure of a route to exit and adequate cash resources

It is one of the saddest scenes in nature. On a deserted beach, mother turtle struggles up the sand, and laboriously digs a hole to lay her eggs. Sometime later, hundreds of tiny baby turtles scramble out and start heading down the beach towards the water. Birds are in a frenzy scooping up such an easy meal. That any make it to the water is a miracle, but once they're there, it's still not safe. Fish start gobbling them up. Of the tiny few that sneak by, some survive to adulthood, and the turtle species lives on.

A world of heartache and loss

That scene reminds me of the business world. The big business names that are so familiar to us, came from somewhere. These 'big turtles' were once just someone's brainwave and ambition. To get to where they are now they needed many things to go well, just to survive. For every big survivor there are countless more that never made it. In addition, these failures caused many people endless heartache and financial loss.

This is the world you become involved in if you invest in private companies. The risks are very high, but so are the potential rewards. As we have seen, I believe that the best trade-off for an investor is with small companies, and because of that, I also believe that private companies can offer fantastic opportunities. An investor, however, must be able to find a way to eventually make a return on his money by selling his shares. That normally requires the company listing on the share market or being bought by another company. To make it to a listing or an acquisition, the company is going to have to survive many difficulties, and will need cash resources to grow and become profitable.

The company life cycle

To understand the challenge, we need to look at the life cycle of a company.

Let's start at the beginning. People start a business for many different reasons. The reason could be an invention, an idea, a perceived opportunity or nothing much more than desire and hope. Often at that point, the financing is with cash from savings, and help from family and friends. It is usually hard to convince banks or other financiers to lend money for a brand new business.

It would be unusual for a new company to become profitable very quickly. So, a race begins between diminishing cash and growing opportunity. If the opportunities grow well enough, the business will have the strength to attract business angels or venture capitalists. Negotiations begin. The new investors will often want a higher level of discipline in the business. They like to have projections, budgets, proper reporting and business plans. They may also insist on management and staff changes. Sometimes they might insist on the founder of the business being moved away from a management position, to focus on their best skill, such as design or sales. It may be felt that the founder is not a good manager of people, or lacks experience in taking companies to the next stage.

Arguments between investors and company founders

Even with an injection of discipline, most businesses still fail even after the business angels or venture capitalists get involved. Sometimes it can turn ugly if there are arguments with the founder over the direction of the business. Both sides can be adamant that they are right. The founder may feel that the money people really know nothing about the clothing or hospitality business, or whatever. The financiers, usually involved in a host of other companies, may feel that the founder is not aware of the bigger picture, such as the general business environment. There can also be arguments between the different investors over the direction of the business.

Further rounds of funding

If the business does survive though, it will often need even further injections of funding, particularly if it looks viable but is not yet profitable. These funds may be needed for expansion, perhaps by the hiring of more people or by the increasing of the marketing budget. Even though the business is still unlisted, it has a share price, and this can rise and fall from funding round to funding round. So there are further discussions and negotiations with the existing investors and potential new investors. The founders may find that they own a smaller and smaller percentage of the company that they started. It may be hard for them to accept that because there is less risk, owning a small part of a big pie, may be better than owning a big part of a small pie.

The process of finding private funding can be dangerous

It is quite a common experience for loss making, cash-stretched businesses to be victims of what I consider immoral behaviour by some investors. An investor will look at the business, and give very warm signals that they wish to invest at a reasonable share price. The investor then drags out the due diligence process of verifying the company's claims, for perhaps several months. Meanwhile, the company's cash resources continue to dwindle, but it feels safe knowing the investment is coming.

Then the crunch happens. The investor dramatically drops the share price that they are willing to pay. Sometimes they spuriously claim that they have found something worrying in the due diligence. By now, the company has backed itself into a corner. It does not have enough cash to start new drawn-out negotiations with different investors, so it has little choice but to accept the deal on the table. It's been screwed! I have warned companies that this can happen, and that even big, well-known fund managers use these tricks.

A less dangerous, but costly experience can occur when new investors buy shares and get added rights over the existing shares. These rights may allow the investor to be protected if the company fails or doesn't meet its forecasts. Certain events will trigger an adjustment process where the investor is given more shares for free, lowering their price per share. One trigger, for example, could be when a company misses a sales forecast. Some companies underestimate the true cost of these small print details, because the trigger events happen quite frequently.

The exit route must always be kept in mind

Anyway, let's hope a fair deal can be reached and there is new investment in the business. The professional investors will be keen to find some exit for their investment. It is unlikely that these type of investors want to receive dividends or slow capital growth. They are typically specialists in the risky end of the market, so that when a business matures, they want to sell their shares and invest in other new opportunities. For them to achieve this exit, the business will need to be bought by another company, or to list on a share market. It will often be a condition of their investment that the business is run with an exit in mind.

Try to be attractive

Positioning a business to be bought is a management skill.

Businesses tend to buy other businesses for two familiar reasons: fear or greed. Fear could cause them to buy a potential competitor. Greed could cause them to buy another company which has moved into markets of interest.

So the strategy is to be attractive to potential buyers. The small business, with its limited resources, may have to choose which products or markets it develops. It can't go after everything. Being attractive may involve decisions which diverge from normal business, so there is some risk involved.

A benefit of being bought, is that it can happen relatively early in the company life cycle. It could occur even before the company has profits or much revenue.

Flotation

On the other hand, listing on the stock market normally requires that a company has profits or genuine prospects in the near term. The process can involve great expense, planning and management time. The ability to float is not just about the company - it also depends on stock market conditions at the time. Normally, a bull market, of some degree, is needed to get companies floated because it gives more confidence to new investors. A float may take up to six months to orchestrate, and market conditions can change greatly in that time, resulting in the float being cancelled. So even if a company is doing quite well, all of the effort and expense could be wasted.

The listing process usually involves the appointment of a broker to facilitate the whole thing. The flotation is normally combined with a funding round, i.e. the initial public offering (or IPO). The broker will introduce the company to big institutional funds who may invest in the round. To be an attractive investment, the company may need to focus on what is fashionable at the time, such as the software in a product rather than the hardware. After gauging the level of interest, the broker may try to argue down the price of the shares for the round. They want the shares to trade higher after the float, so that their institutions, who have invested, make a profit. Even though it is the company that pays a healthy fee to the broker, it is really the institutions that keep the brokers going.

Another thing the broker may push for are lock-ins, where the founders, and perhaps other shareholders, agree not to sell shares for some period of time. It is easier for the broker to promote shares in a company if the important people are staying involved.

If the flotation happens, it changes the nature of the ownership. In the first few weeks of trading on the market, there can be big volumes as the early investors - often high-risk investors such as business angels and venture capital funds - sell their shares and other funds come in as buyers.

Be wary of projections in business plans

This life cycle of a company, from conception to a listing on the share market, can take a very long time. New companies often underestimate the amount of cash required to reach profitability and an exit for investors. Of all of the companies I have backed, I cannot remember an initial business plan being achieved. There is an inbuilt asymmetry, as most things can prove to be worse than the plan, but it's hard for them to prove to be better than the plan. I have now adopted a loose methodology of doubling the time and cost of any projections that people give me.

In summary, when investing in an unlisted company, you need to take a view on your ability to exit. There are many different things for the company to accomplish, and it will rarely be smooth sailing. Ensuring that the company has adequate cash resources will usually be one of the challenges.

6.8 Shareholders can help unlisted companies

I have explained the challenges that face unlisted companies in their quest towards profitability and an exit for investors. For these companies, the shareholders can add value to the business. They may add strength to the management by lending their experience and expertise. They can also be very useful in building relationships with other companies, since, of course, the business world is mostly about networking and friendships. For these reasons, when I am considering an investment in an unlisted company, I usually make some effort to know a little about the expertise and attitude of other investors.

Analyse your fellow shareholders

When I first invested in the private members' club, Home House, part of my reasoning was based on the strength of the other shareholders. Other investors included a number of very successful people from the restaurant business, and a number of others who were very successful in the construction business. I had absolutely no experience or skill in either of those areas. There was no way I could evaluate the opportunity in the same way as those people. I considered their willingness to invest as a big vote of confidence in the project. I also knew that their involvement going forward would be invaluable. This thinking proved to be spot on, and the strength of the investor expertise was probably the biggest factor in achieving the phenomenal success of the club.

I have also used this type of logic for technology investments. Again, although I make my own judgement on the quality of the management and the other criteria discussed in this chapter, I have no comparative advantage whatsoever in assessing the technology. So it gives me some comfort when I co-invest with, say, an investment fund that employs experts on the technology.

Other shareholders can also be vital to help future financing needs of the company. This is particularly important for small companies that may need expansion capital or emergency capital if things don't go as well as hoped or planned (which is not unusual!).

On the other hand, bad shareholders can cause many difficulties for a small company. I have often seen this up close. On one occasion, I saw a shareholder hold up the sale of a company by trying to get a better price per share than everybody else, even though it was in his interests to accept the existing offer. He figured that as he was a small part of the transaction, he could hold the larger shareholders to ransom. Fortunately, he was persuaded by the threat to his reputation as word spread of his actions.

On another occasion, I negotiated the sale of a business in consultation with the other shareholders. When I shook hands on the deal with the buyer, one shareholder then demanded and was able to achieve, better terms for himself. He behaved unethically by pretending that he was united with the rest of the shareholders, when really he was just gleaning information. That's business, you might say, but it shows that it's a good idea to assess your partners.

Even when investing in listed companies, it can still be useful to know the identity of the other shareholders. A friend of mine, Didi, likes to monitor and invest in small NASDAQ stocks. He takes a lot of notice when good quality fund managers invest in these stocks. He uses his own judgement when investing, but also watches the other investors who are better placed than him to assess the company. With this verification of his own view he has performed very well.

6.9 Be pragmatic with due diligence

Investing in private companies involves extra risks. Often the companies are involved in new markets with new products, and it is difficult to assess their true chances. There is also less protection against fraud for investors, because the unlisted market is not as regulated as the listed market.

Consequently, there can be a greater need for an investor to perform due diligence before investing. This is the process of checking out a company's claims, and the viability of its markets. For many venture capitalists investing in private companies, the due diligence can be extensive and take months. They will do things such as test products, check patents, check customer references, interview staff and look at bank statements.

Is it necessary to do so much homework before investing?

How do you spell chip?

In my early days, I did make some effort to learn as much as I could about a company before I invested, and to check their claims. However, I have never been particularly good at this process. Getting involved in all of the detail does not exactly thrill me. What's more, although I have backed many technology companies, I don't know much about technology.

I have often joked that I can barely spell 'chip', let alone understand how they work. I could also say that if I ever understand a technology, I shouldn't invest, because it's obviously not that clever!

To truly understand technology, you need to be trained as something like an electrical engineer or a physicist. It is constantly evolving, which is why it's exciting and offers fantastic investment opportunities. But that makes it hard to keep up-to-date. For those reasons, I admire managers without a technical background who lead technology companies. They have learnt a lot on the job.

Trust the managers

Over the years my approach to due diligence has become more pragmatic. I usually verify the honesty and ability of the management by meeting them face to face and by looking at their track records. It is unlikely that someone with a good career will suddenly become fraudulent. Once I am satisfied that they're honest and capable, I usually accept their view on their company's product and on the prospects in the market place. This is where I diverge from more conservative investors and most venture capitalists.

In general, I do not believe that investors need to be experts in everything about the company. In fact, for some things, it is better to assume that you know nothing. I have often heard investors making judgements on things when they are frankly, not qualified. I rarely back my individual view on technology. How can I assess a company that produces drugs for treating cancer? It is better to take a view on the quality of the management and their team, and to trust their judgement. There is an even stronger argument for this approach when they have a strong stake in the company's success, via shares or options.

Apart from assessing the management, I will make some superficial enquiries with technical experts from other companies with which I am involved. Often the experts disagree anyway. I have asked engineers about technologies and some have been big fans and others very negative. In addition, of course, I will have a quick look at existing sales levels, customer interest and other contacts that the company has generated, as signs that their product is viable.

The benefits of this 'I trust you' approach to due diligence, apart from saving a lot of energy, are that:

1. I can often invest very quickly, and this speed sometimes allows me to negotiate a much lower price.

2. I can invest in companies where it is difficult to verify managements claims. Again, this can provide an opportunity for me to achieve a lower price, because other potential investors may shy away from these opportunities, leaving me with less competition for the deal.

Radiation Watch

Recently I met with a company which was looking for capital to expand its business. The venture capital funds had been playing games, and the company were prepared to offer me attractive terms to get a deal done.

The company, Radiation Watch Ltd, had designed a wearable device that monitors radiation levels with digital feedback and wireless communication. It is ground-breaking technology which could revolutionise radiation detection. The managers started the business, and in their opinion the nearest competitor is about eighteen months behind.

Although the product is still in development, there are many potential buyers. The technology could obviously be of interest to the US government for homeland security and defence. For example, they could equip police cars with kits so that the police could quickly measure potential radiation threats.

In addition, hospitals, nuclear facilities and other users of radiation have indicated that they would have an interest in the wearable devices. So there is the possibility of Radiation Watch grabbing big shares in these markets.

I was very impressed with the four managers. They had been recommended by an industry contact, and I knew that they had each enjoyed successful business careers. Consequently, their commitment to Radiation Watch demonstrated that they believed it was a genuine opportunity. They were to maintain a significant shareholding in the business, and would remain fully motivated. I also felt comfortable that I would be able to approach them at any time for an informal update on business progress.

With a share price valuing the company in the low millions, I was happy to commit, after one meeting, to an investment of over half a million pounds. There was nothing fancy about the deal, I would simply buy shares in the business. So we agreed to instruct the lawyers to keep it plain and simple.

The meeting took just over one hour, and that was the extent of my due diligence. I was able to move quickly on an investment when other investors wanted to take months.

7 Price Behaviour

7.0 Prices go further than expected

This is one of the most important Strategies in this book. Historically, all of the different asset classes have a habit of surprising people by how far they move, and by how long they keep moving. While the market also has plenty of periods when it goes nowhere, the small moves do not come as a surprise. The amazing thing is the price reaction when the fundamentals change.

As a trader and an investor, if you can develop the habit of sticking with winning positions, you can obtain a significant comparative advantage. You will find that long after many others have sold out prematurely, you can persist, even if you are amazed by the market's subsequent performance.

My longest trade

The biggest price move that I have captured was in the Australian government bond market. The fall in interest rates that started in 1989 and lasted until 1993 exceeded all of my expectations. During that period, ten year yields fell from nearly 14% to under 7%, as bonds enjoyed a dramatic bull market.

I managed to stay invested for almost the entire move and made great profits. Around me, I saw many other traders doing things differently. Some tried to fight the move and lost money. Others had the right view on the fundamentals but did not make big profits, because all they did was grab an odd half a per cent here and there.

Stay with the winners – don't get shaken out

The big moves provide fantastic opportunities to make money. It is necessary to avoid the temptation to jump on and off a good idea in just a week or a month, and to instead doggedly stay with the winners.

To convince you about the size of some market moves and the lengths of time involved, let's look at some very well-known examples. All of these were big moves over a number of years, and few people expected them.

- The **Dow Jones Industrial Average** had an almost uninterrupted run in the 1990s when it rose from under 3,000 to over 11,000 by the end of the decade.

- **Gold** had a big fall from $400 in the mid 1990s to about $250 in 1999 before moving higher to $400 by end 2003.

- **Crude** oil has had some big moves. Driven by OPEC and events in Iran and Iraq, the oil price rose from a few dollars per barrel in 1970 to over $35 by the early 1980s. It then collapsed to under $10 per barrel by December 1988. With the Iraqi invasion of Kuwait and the Gulf War, the price spiked to over $38 in 1990. Improved drilling and production techniques in the 1990s saw the price fall to below $10 by 1999. With the troubles in Iraq it then rose close to $50 in 2004 and climbed to over $60 in 2005 with Hurricane Katrina. A roller coaster ride by any standards.

- **Currencies** too, have had some incredible shifts. In early 1984, 1 dollar bought about 250 yen. Now it buys less than 110 yen. After the euro started trading as a theoretical currency in January 1999, it sank from a first day high of nearly $1.20 to around $0.80 about two years later. It then recovered to over $1.30 in early 2005. It is astounding that the world's most important exchange rates can have such big moves.

- **Housing prices** are estimated to have more than doubled during 1997 to 2004 in the UK and Australia, and nearly tripled in Ireland. In the US, the rise has been a more modest 60% or so. Who would have thought that these moves could happen? Not the economists, property experts or the press.

These are the types of opportunities that should appeal to you. If you can correctly identify the changes in the fundamentals, you may have plenty of time to take a position and enjoy a very favourable move in the price. Over the years, by recognising that prices go further than expected, I have been very good at staying on winning ideas. Long after many others have sold out of winning positions, I have persisted, even though I have been amazed by how far the market subsequently went.

7.1 Forget the old price

People often arbitrarily decide that a market is under or overvalued. In many cases, it is based on a feeling that the price has moved too far. However, this is an unreliable technique in the markets.

"Ridiculous oil"

In 2005 I chatted to a friend of mine about the price of oil, which had just broken through $45 per barrel. We had opposite views on the market. To me, oil was a case where the fundamentals were all bullish. A checklist on the oil price at the time only had pluses, and included things such as:

- the tensions in Iraq and the Middle East in general;
- instability in Nigeria;
- low levels of US inventory; and
- the steady increase in demand from China and the rest of Asia.

If you added to these fundamentals the upward trend in the price, you got a market where everything pointed in the same direction: higher prices. Given that prices go further than expected, I would not have been surprised to see a big move upwards.

On the other hand, my friend's view was that $45 per barrel was "ridiculous"! His bearish view was completely based on the idea that the price had come too far from its earlier levels. In the middle of 2003, it was only a touch over $20.

However, I was puzzled by his logic. At any price above, say, $30 it could be argued that oil had come a long way from around $20. Therefore, if his trading methodology is to bet against big moves, he would have been bearish while the price rose steadily to $45. He could easily have been behind by more than $15 per barrel already.

Which price is wrong?

I thought there was another weakness in his logic. If a big move means that the market has made a mistake, is the old price or the new price the wrong one? Oil could have been ridiculous at $20, rather than at $45.

I frequently hear or read comments that suggest a market has gone too far, and that a price is unsustainable. I would definitely not invest or trade on that kind of thinking. We need something more logical and reliable. With that in mind, forget the old price, and expect prices to go a long way.

As I write, oil sits above $60.

7.2 People often misjudge probability and logic

Most of us are actually poor judges of probability. We are not really focussed on assessing different possibilities or on keeping an open mind. To start with, it is human nature to seek clarity. No one likes to be wishy-washy, so we make up our minds about things. "America is good." "America is bad." "Arsenal will beat Manchester United." "That business will make millions." Being definitive about things has its benefits, but it can stop us thinking clearly about different possibilities and probabilities.

Errors involving simple logic

Sometimes we have problems with simple logic. I know married friends who do not travel on the same aeroplane when their children are not with them, because they don't want to leave them as orphans if there is a plane crash. However, as a couple without the children, they will often travel together in a car on a motorway, which at high speed is far more risky.

As a more trivial example, you may have seen surveys taken by television stations where viewers are asked to phone and vote about a topical issue. The weakness is of course, that most people do not bother, and those that do, normally have a particular axe to grind. So when a station reports that say, 75% of people are in favour of higher nurses' pay, there is a good chance that most of the yes votes are simply from nurses themselves, or people who are especially sympathetic to nurses. Many viewers may think that the level of nurses' pay is just fine, but they are not as strongly inclined to pick up the phone, and their votes are not counted. This is a classic case of a biased sample, because the voters do not represent the entire community. The results are meaningless.

High profile events are overestimated

High profile events can skew peoples' views of reality. Because some events attract publicity, it is easy to overestimate the odds involved. We all focus on the lottery winner more than the thousands or millions of ticket buyers who quietly miss out.

Parents see famous sports people and push their kids hard towards that goal. It's a lousy bet, but they don't think about the number of failures. Concentrating on schoolwork gives much better odds of making a decent living. In Monaco, I have seen a young girl forced by her mother to practise tennis, even though the girl was in tears as she was playing. If the mother thought about the real odds of her daughter winning Wimbledon, she might just let the little girl spend more time having fun - or doing homework.

Unusual events do happen

On the other hand, people underestimate how often unexpected events occur. Unlikely things do happen, and when they do, it is human nature to look for another cause apart from what's obvious. This creates conspiracy theories. People assume that there must be more than simple explanations for the death of Princess Diana or JFK.

Traps for investors

In the markets, these kinds of mistakes can be dangerous. A common pitfall is to overestimate the strategies we see employed by successful investors. Again, the success stories may just be the tip of the iceberg. There might be a large number of investors who have failed pursuing the same strategies, and their failures are not so visible. George Soros may be famous as a successful currency speculator, but there are many other investors who have lost a lot of money trading currencies. So if a friend of yours makes money by starting his own business, before you follow in his footsteps, think about the very high failure rate suffered by new businesses.

This logic is often missed in articles and books that analyse successful investors. They survey millionaires to find out all kinds of things, like what areas they invest in, what sort of school they went to, what they ate as a baby or what star sign they are. Then they use the results to explain why having a particular characteristic helps to make you a millionaire. Ignore these conclusions, they're rubbish. You have to include the non-millionaires in the sample to get to the truth.

Hindsight and over-confidence

Another danger is, that in retrospect the financial markets can seem quite simple. It's easy to think that the bursting of the tech bubble was bound to happen because of the crazy valuations, or that the dollar was bound to fall because of the high trade deficit. We forget that at the time, most of us were very uncertain about what was going to happen. That's why so few people made money from these 'obvious' price moves.

It's important not to allow the comfort of hindsight to make you overconfident. The investor doesn't have the luxury of becoming too sure of their views. If they fall for that trap, they will soon come unstuck.

For this reason, I try to keep an open mind, even when I am asked for my views on the markets. Normally, of course, what is wanted is a simple view of up or down. However, I don't allow myself to think of prices in that way. As I have explained, I have a lot of respect for the existing price and the market's ability to act like a super computer. I think there is only a small chance of outguessing it. I believe that it is essential to see markets from both sides, and to understand how prices are based on probabilities.

That is the subject of the next three Strategies.

7.3 A price is an average of possibilities

When I first started working in financial markets I used to look at prices as I'd been taught in economics - supply and demand produce a price. Changes to supply and demand then change that price. This reasoning is, of course, correct, but it doesn't deal specifically with randomness.

I eventually taught myself to think more and more of prices being the result of a random process, where the price has some chance of going up, and some of going down. In some cases, I became interested in trying to put an actual percentage on these probabilities.

Calculating price probabilities

Let's say a central bank is considering raising interest rates by half of a per cent - 50 basis points. The market rate may already be 30 points higher, as it starts to price-in the rate rise possibility. To me, this represents a 60% chance that there will be a rate increase and 40% of no change.

Now, if I thought that there was a greater chance of the rise than the market's 60%, I could take a position that way, and hope for the rate rise to happen.

Note that there is no mention of supply and demand in this analysis. It's just an assumption that two things can happen, and estimating their chances. I started thinking this way in the 80s and now have the satisfaction of hearing more and more analysts talking in these terms.

But you can't be too precise

Although in my example I've given specific percentages, it's not normally possible to be that exact. Usually it's more a feeling and a vague notion – a rough idea of the chances of the market rising by x, or falling by y. Trying to be more precise than that involves spurious accuracy.

As an example of my approach, I have just invested in a company because, in my view, the chances of the price doing well are about 2 in 3, with only about 1 in 3 of it doing badly.

The current price is bound to move one way or another

Seeing prices in terms of these simple probabilities opens up a new way of thinking. You may realise, for example, that *sometimes the current price is unsustainable.* In these cases, the price has a chance of going up and a chance of going down, but virtually zero of staying the same. In the rate rise example I have given, the market price is set to move one way or another after the central bank decision. It will not ignore the information. A small company hoping to win an important order will see its stock price move higher or lower after the announcement. The price will not stay the same, because the news will be too big to ignore.

I have made use of unsustainable prices by using techniques in the options markets, which I will discuss later. By buying put and call options simultaneously, I have been able to make profits, not having a clue about which way the price was going, but by simply knowing that it would move significantly one way or the other.

7.4 The probability can be asymmetric

In the US led invasion of Iraq in 2003, there was a great deal of uncertainty, and the world nervously watched and waited as the tanks rolled in.

If events went relatively smoothly, Saddam would be ousted, an Arab democracy created, and western oil supply solidified.

If events went badly, there could be an absolute disaster, with the use of weapons of mass destruction, millions of refugees, an Arab-Israeli war, or terrorist attacks in the west matching September 11th, 2001.

Without discussing the merits of the war, I believed at the time that there was a much greater chance of events going well. If they did, stock markets would trade higher after the invasion. Now did this mean that I was a keen buyer of the market? Quite simply, no.

The scenario at that time is illustrated in the graph. The stock market would probably rise by a small amount following a successful invasion. But this did not represent a buying opportunity because it would fall by a far greater amount in the less likely event of a disaster. It was nothing more than a fair bet.

Stock prices scenario

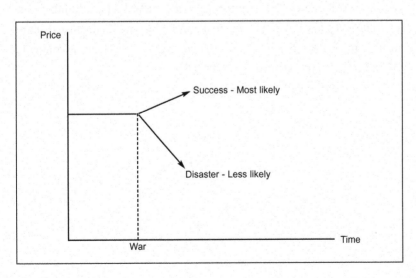

This is what I call an *asymmetric situation*, it occurs when a market is more likely to move in one direction than the other. This is balanced out by the different sizes of the potential moves.

I started thinking about this after learning to look at prices in terms of probabilities. I was fascinated by the rather paradoxical idea that markets which will *probably* rally are not always a buying opportunity.

It is important to recognise when you are involved in an asymmetric situation. Be careful when the market is awaiting important events such as economic releases, and especially events of the magnitude of the Iraq war. The odds may be that you can correctly judge the outcome, but the potential losses if you are wrong could be larger than the potential profits.

Some markets perennially go up slowly and down quickly

The share market at that time was an asymmetric market because of the approaching war. Some markets are asymmetric all of the time. This especially applies to those where the yield is high or low.

Take junk bonds, for example. These are loan instruments issued by lower grade companies which are viewed as having more chance of defaulting. They pay a high yield to compensate investors for that higher risk. Normally, there is steady buying interest due to the attraction of the higher yield, and the price can drift higher. Any selling pressure tends to be around crises, which by their very nature are unexpected and immediate, and cause a sharp drop in the price. An example of a crisis could be when a company announces that it is not performing very well.

This produces a price pattern of smooth rises punctuated by sharp falls.

Asymmetric Market

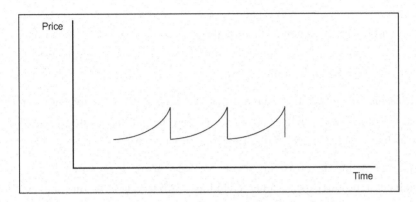

The pattern inspired the expression, 'up by the fire stairs, down by the elevator shaft' to describe the asymmetry of the Australian dollar in the 1980s, when Australian interest rates were relatively high. You can see that asymmetric markets tends to have smooth moves in one direction, with occasional sharp moves in the opposite direction.

Asymmetric markets are a danger. If you are backing the smoother direction, you can grow comfortable over a period of time as the market drifts in your favour. However this may be brought to a sudden end with a big thud and a nasty reversal. It is also difficult to try to bet on the less predictable reversals, as you may wait a long time.

7.5 Be nervous when a market doesn't rally on good news

First, we need some background. A market's response to news is normally all about expectations. In the time leading up to a news event (e.g. the release of an economic statistic), analysts, economists and other players build up expectations about the outcome. By the time the statistic is released, the price has largely built in the expected result. For the market then, a 'good' or 'bad' number means the number was better or worse than the expectation.

Naturally this is very well-known in the markets. It is why there is so much interest in the forecasts of statistics before their release. A company may announce a big rise in profits, but the stock price can still fall if the market had been *expecting* an even better result.

If buyers don't want to buy when there is good news, when will they?

I have, of course, been watching news announcements and the market reaction for years. Over that time I have grown more confident that the market's subsequent behaviour can be a useful indicator of its future path. If there is a favourable announcement and the market doesn't rally, it can be a sell signal. Equally, if there is an unfavourable announcement and the market doesn't weaken, it can be a buy signal.

One reason for this Strategy operating is, if buyers don't want to buy when there is good news, when will they? You may be waiting a long time. A similar logic applies if sellers don't emerge on bad news.

This Strategy has been useful to me over the years. Most often, I have combined it to finesse my other techniques. After watching the market's response to a news announcement, I may add to a winning position, or cut a losing position before my stop-loss is reached. In all cases, I still, of course, watch the fundamentals in case of a change in my underlying views.

I am even more confident if the market responds in the same fashion to a series of news announcements. I remember a number of years ago that I was quite impressed when the share market brushed off a whole host of poor profit figures over a few weeks. It then went on to rise strongly over the following months.

7.6 Don't day trade!

Day trading refers to buying and selling within one day, so that you end the day with no position, only your cash profit or loss. A lot of people do it, even amateurs – for as long as they survive. It can be very exciting for some people, because the thrill to them is similar to gambling.

This is probably a good place to give a warning.

After my earlier discussions about big picture ideas and markets moving further than expected, the thought of buying something in the morning to sell it in the afternoon, should seem ridiculous.

I am interested in things that take time to play out, and I have never made money out of day trading. In fact, I have rarely made money out of any quick trade.

Only day trade if you are at the coalface

The only people I know who have really had success with day trading are people at the coalface. These have been people working on the floor of an exchange or at a broking house. There, they can see the build up of orders and make a quick guess of what's going to happen over the next few hours. With that information, they can make money. There were many comical stories that used to come out of the floor of the Sydney Futures Exchange before it went electronic. The traders would try to spy on each other to see who was buying or selling. This led to all sorts of cloak and dagger subterfuge such as special passwords, secret sign language and fake order books. They had fun.

You and I don't have the information to make a sensible assessment of what's going to happen to a price over a day, or even a month or longer. The opportunities we seek are offered by big picture influences, and they take longer to play out.

7.7 Avoid trading in options if you do not understand their pricing

Options can be very useful in a wide variety of markets. A potential buyer of a property may look to buy an option for a small sum, so that they have the right to buy the property if they can raise the funds, but not the obligation, in case they can't. Staff options over company shares can be given to employees for free, and are great motivators since they can become very valuable if the company does well.

For trading and investing, options can be a very powerful instrument if you know what you are doing. They can provide fantastic leverage, since the cost of the option may be a fraction of the cost of the underlying asset. They can also be a very good way of limiting risk, as the maximum loss when you buy an option is limited to that cost.

The difficulty with options, on the other hand, is in deciding what they are worth. Clearly, the longer the time to expiry, and the more volatile the market, the more valuable the option, but by how much? It is not always easy to just guess the answer. People outside of the financial world normally have absolutely no idea. I have been involved in a number of company restructures where, understandably, people have struggled to find the right mix for the staff options. Usually I have had to fix the mess created by accountants or lawyers who have gone astray with their methodology.

It is not just laymen who have problems with options, because even people in the financial arena frequently struggle. I have seen many traders lose money because they simply didn't know what they were doing. For this reason I do not think it is a good idea for ordinary investors to trade options, unless they make some effort to understand their value.

Fortunately, for those who want it, there is a way forward. In the remainder of this Strategy, I am going to present a very simple approach I have developed for pricing options. It has proved very popular with my team and other traders.

It's not difficult, but please skip this section if you feel options are not for you.

A simple approach to option pricing

The standard method for calculating option prices is based on a method using the Black Scholes model, which was devised by Fischer Black and Myron Scholes, and for which they won the Nobel Prize in Economics. Unfortunately, the mathematics is nowhere near straightforward, and in using the model, you run the risk of not knowing what implicit assumptions you are making.

Early in my career, I made the effort to learn the options pricing models, but I did not use them for trading. I simply never felt confident with the black box approach. So I soon developed a system that is far simpler and easier to understand. What also appeals to me is that you can see exactly what you are doing. You are not obliged to use an implied symmetrical bell-shaped curve or anything like that!

To explain how it works, it is easiest to use an example. Remember that an option is the right to buy or sell something in the future at a fixed price. The fixed price is known as the 'exercise price' or the 'strike price' and the cost to buy the option as the 'premium'. Options to buy are known as 'calls' and to sell as 'puts'.

Let's say a market is trading at a price of 100, and you want to value an option to buy in six months at 110. This is an 'out of the money' option, because if you exercised it today, it would be worthless. It has no 'intrinsic value'. What it does have is 'time value' because if the price moves above 110 before maturity, it will be worth something.

My valuation process takes a simple view of the world. All you need to do is to choose some levels where the price could be in six months, and give each of them a percentage probability. The answer after that is quite simple. Have a look at the following table:

(1) Possible Prices	(2) Percentage Probability	(3) Return $=110-(1)$	(4) Weighted Return $=(2) * (3)$
60	5	0	0
80	10	0	0
100	50	0	0
120	30	10	3
140	5	30	1.5
	Total = 100	Option Value	= 4.5

In Column (1), I have used prices going up and down from the current level by intervals of 20. In Column (2) is the judgement call - here I have chosen my percentage probabilities. These must add up to 100.

Column (3) is the return from the call option for each price. At prices of 110 or less, this is zero, and at higher prices it starts to have value. That value would be obtained by exercising the option and immediately selling the asset back into the marketplace. Obviously, the value can never be negative because you are not forced to exercise the option. Column (4) is obtained by multiplying the percentage probability and the return, to give us a 'weighted return'.

By taking the sum of the weighted returns, we find the implied option value. It is a simple methodology really, and it's not going to win me a Nobel Prize, but I love the transparency and intuitiveness. It is easy to play around with the subjective percent probabilities and see what happens to the option value.

There are a few things to note. You can put in more and more possible outcomes for Column (1), which would increase the accuracy if you were sure of their probabilities. In my experience though, you only have a feel for a few different points rather than very many. The other thing is that it may be a good idea to check your weighted expected price, which is found by multiplying Column (1) and Column (2) and summing the results. If this is vastly different from the current price, your probabilities are very bullish or bearish, so be sure that is your intention.

I have not mentioned interest costs for the model. If the option has a long maturity, remember that you should allow for the loss of interest due to paying for the premium at the outset.

Now the idea is, that you can run the model and compare your valuation to what the options cost in the market. If they cost less, you may want to buy some. I have often used the model in this way to identify successful trading opportunities.

Buying options is one thing, but I would not recommend to readers at this stage that they consider selling options. Since prices often go further than expected, it is easy to misjudge the probabilities. Selling options also involves high risk for only a limited return, and requires very good risk management.

7.8 Back your hunches with a small investment at least

Some things are just as true in trading as they are in life, such as:

- There is no substitute for experience.
- It is easy to underestimate what you will learn once you get involved in something.
- Things have a habit of looking simple until you really try them.

Most things I have learnt about trading have started with a vague idea that interested me, which I have then pursued and learnt more about once I was involved.

Get involved

My involvement in small companies started exactly that way. In the mid 1990s, I thought that the stock market was due for a rally and I had a hunch that small stocks offered good opportunities. I started with small amounts and made many mistakes. For example, I didn't know what 'due diligence' was, and I trusted everybody. However, if I had never started, I would never have learnt anything. As it was, I was able to make contacts and increase my skills. Before that I had no idea how involved I would become, or how many opportunities were genuinely there.

Similarly, when I started investigating market behaviour in the late 1980s, I had no idea that it would lead to a trading model that we would use 24 hours a day on markets all over the world. The original idea was just to use the research to trade the markets after economic announcements, but we learnt more than that and it led to other ideas.

So I have learnt to back all of my hunches with at least a small investment, even if it's just a tiny position to see what happens. Obviously, I still use these Strategies to help form a view and to trade the positions.

Paper trading is not a substitute

Having real positions is completely different to 'paper trading', where you pretend to invest and you keep some score on how you would perform. With paper trading, you do not have any pressure, and the motivation is not the same.

Another benefit of backing all of your hunches, is that it is very frustrating to miss a winning idea. At least if you put something on an idea and it loses, you usually learn something. If you miss a winner, you may not learn anything, and you've missed an opportunity.

7.9 Features of good trading models

I have had a lot of experience with models (I mean trading models, not fashion models!). Trading models are the holy grail of finance. The models use clear-cut rules on when to buy and sell. They have the lure of being nice and easy to operate once they have been designed. There is no straining over fundamentals and stressing over when to do the trades.

Different types of trading models

There are many different types of trading models. Some are based on very simple rules, such as buying stocks in December and selling them in January. Some look at the relationships between different markets, such as between interest rates and the share market. Others use the state of the economy and economic statistics. Models that are more complicated could use a combination of the market and economic inputs. What they all have in common is the assumption that a trading rule based on historical success will continue to perform in the future.

My involvement with models goes back to when I worked briefly at Australia's central bank and we were working on an economic model of Australia. It was ambitious stuff, but the aim was to see how the economy responded to changes in interest rates and other variables. Later, I became very interested in trading models and I started to design them at Bankers Trust.

So when one fellow came to the bank with a trading model, he was sent to see me. He wanted us to use his system on the stock market and to pay him a percentage of any profits. He showed me a price chart with lots of buys and sells written on it, and it looked good. The buys were nearly always below the sells, and it would have made a great return. However, I didn't accept his offer, because I was not satisfied that the model had what I consider to be the essential features of a good trading model:

- A sound explanation for its success;
- Involvement of only limited testing on historical data; and
- Simplicity.

The need for an underlying theory

The process of designing a model should start with an underlying theory, which is then tested with the data. In other words, the data should be used to check a theory, not to find one. If a model does not have an underlying explanation or logic, I am very doubtful that it will work.

Be wary of data mining

The ease of designing trading models has been made vastly easier with computers. Almost any idea can be tested on historical data to check its profitability. This has led to an explosion in 'data mining' - running zillions of tests on all sorts of data in the search for some trading rule that works.

I am very much against data mining. If you continue mining all sorts of data, you *will* find something, but it will probably just be based on coincidence. It may be a very odd rule, based on phases of the moon, what you had for breakfast, or something equally ridiculous.

So the searching through historical data should be limited. You are more confident if you have one idea, test it and it works, rather than if you run a thousand ideas and stumble across some coincidence. Remember there is an assumption that patterns which occurred in the past will occur again. We are not looking for crazy coincidences but for repeating behaviour.

Keep it simple

The simpler the design of the model, the more powerful. I distrust models that are overly complicated. Because markets are a product of human behaviour, it is unlikely that they follow an unknown but precise pattern.

In the following chapters, I am going to outline a simple model that I designed to identify and trade markets that move in trends. In designing the model, I was very disciplined and I selected the exact parameters before I ran any tests. When I saw the results - eureka! - I found the model would have been profitable over the test period. Then, I did not try for improvements by changing the parameters and re-running the data. In this way, I maintained confidence that the model would work in the future and was not a fluke result.

8 The Understanding and Use of Trends in Prices

8.0 There is statistical proof that market prices trend

I remember vividly the day in the late 80s when I was first able to prove statistically that most market prices move in trends. I was absolutely flabbergasted, and really pleased. Here I had found a gift. Price moves could be partially predicted!

For quite some time I had suspected that prices trend, and my trading style had already evolved so that I traded with a trend, rather than against one. I preferred to buy when the market was already rising because I sensed that I was swimming with the tide. I also had some ideas as to *why* prices should trend.

Blind Freddy loves charts

However, without proof, I could not be certain. Although Blind Freddy could spot big sweeping moves upwards and downwards on most price charts, I knew that charts could play tricks with the mind. We can fail to spot the occasions where prices start to move in one direction but then turn around. It can be very expensive for a trader to buy a rising market if the price does not continue higher and falls back instead.

Of course I also knew that other people were aware of price trends - the famous saying 'the trend is your friend' has been around a long time. However, I had not seen anyone make money out of them. In fact, most people thought it was cleverer to look for opportunities where a market had gone too far, and to bet against a trend. Some people tried to use the charts to trade trends. However, this is a very clumsy way of doing it! And for some reason chartists would not just pursue trends, they would mess things up by looking for other, rather strange patterns as well.

Economics theory suggests trends don't exist

The other thing that worried me was that if trends existed there was an inefficiency in the market. Economic theory suggests that these do not exist.

The price direction in the past should have no bearing whatsoever on the future direction. Your chances should be the same if you buy a falling or a rising market. Trends on the other hand imply that future price moves are not completely random, because they are more likely to follow their existing direction, than to go the other way. Trends are completely inconsistent with the theory.

Trend Trader

So how did I get the proof that I was so keen to find? I designed a basic model called, imaginatively, 'Trend Trader'. With Trend Trader, my team and I ran computer tests using historical data on a broad range of markets. We compared how often markets continued in an existing direction to how often they went into reverse. In theory, the results should be around 50:50 for continuations versus reversals.

However, the exciting thing was that the results showed an average of around 55% continuations to 45% reversals, which is a very strong bias. The difference is a percentage of net winners, 10%.

The figure of 10% is enough to indicate a significant comparative advantage, if it is utilised in the right way. You may remember, I have argued that small percentage advantages can be enough to generate very high returns.

Later in the book, I will discuss how I have successfully used Trend Trader to trade in the markets. The real life results have been consistent with the theoretical results.

The implications of trending markets

When a market is trending up, it is more likely to rise further than it is to fall. Equally, when it is trending down, it is more likely to fall further than it is to rise.

Now what do I mean by trending up and trending down? I mean that a market has had a fairly smooth rise or fall by a meaningful amount. A small move of one or two per cent does not define a trend. These moves may be just 'noise' in the market, caused by the random actions of a few buyers or sellers. A trend requires a more meaningful move, such as five or ten per cent. On this, your instincts will guide you well.

Having a feel for how a market is trending gives us some inkling of what is likely to happen in the future. Statistically it is a good idea to follow the trend. The implication is clear, if you want probability on your side: *buy a rising market, sell a falling market.*

Over the years, my enthusiasm about price trends has not diminished. Trends remain the easiest trading advantage that I have come across. As for any book on the subject of trading which doesn't mention that markets 'tend to trend', throw it away. Trending is too big to ignore, and trends are not an opinion, they are a fact.

With these Strategies I have tried to develop a theory around trends, and I will examine why they exist and why they persist. Strangely, the implications of trends, are ignored (even denied!) by mainstream thinking:

1. Markets tend to under-react, not overreact.

2. Big, obvious ideas offer great opportunities.

3. It is safe to invest with a consensus view.

4. Contrarian trading is usually irrational.

5. It is best to enter and exit markets at the right times instead of always staying invested.

These are ideas that are very important to me. We will see later, that combining an understanding of trends with some understanding of the fundamentals can provide a very powerful trading technique

8.1 Trends operate across commodities, currencies, interest rates, stocks and property

Stirring from a deep sleep one night, I half opened my eyes. The digital clock by the bed showed 4.05am. I watched it change: 4.06...4.07...4.08. Finally, I saw the opportunity: "This market's a buy."

I must have needed a holiday...

Without getting too carried away, it is amazing that markets, on average, trend so strongly. Moreover, it is also amazing that this behaviour is true for nearly all markets. There seem to be very few exceptions. It is extraordinary that trends apply so consistently across many different markets in many different countries.

To see what I mean, have a look at the table overleaf. It gives a sample of some recent results using the model, Trend Trader, I described in the previous Strategy. The '% of net winners' gives an indication of how strongly each market moves in trends. A zero would imply that the market does not trend at all, and is an 'efficient market'. But you can see that just about all of them are positive percentages, and that clearly, trends operate across commodities, currencies, interest rates and stocks. There is only a handful where following trends would cause long term losses, which is when the bias is negative.

I will not go into detail about all the different markets and why some have trended better than others, or why some don't trend at all. Any discussion of small differences between the markets would be meaningless anyway. What is significant is the fact that the vast majority move in trends.

As I have mentioned, the average bias towards the trend direction is about 10%. This may seem like a small number, but it is extremely important - remember that even a small advantage like this is enough to help us tremendously.

Analysis of trending across many different markets

Description	Bias %	Start Date	Last Date
Aluminium (LME)	16.9	11/06/1987	25/07/2003
American Express	3.9	01/04/1977	11/11/2004
Aussie Bills (SFE)	8.98	05/04/1983	25/07/2003
Aussie Bonds 10 Yr (SFE)	11	05/12/1984	25/07/2003
Aussie Dollar (IMM)	11.92	13/01/1987	25/07/2003
Bankers Acceptance (MNTEX)	14.32	13/12/1990	25/07/2003
Boeing	11.94	02/01/1962	11/11/2004
British Pounds (IMM)	13.1	07/12/1983	25/07/2003
Canadian Bond (MNTEX)	5.44	15/09/1989	25/07/2003
Canadian Dollar (IMM)	10.06	01/02/1984	25/07/2003
Coca Cola	7.44	26/03/1990	11/11/2004
Crude Oil (NYMEX)	18.66	15/02/1984	25/07/2003
DAX – Composite	16.08	23/11/1990	14/07/2004
DAX Stock Index (DTB)	17.14	23/11/1990	25/07/2003
Dow Jones	6.96	03/02/1930	17/06/2004
E-Mini NASDAQ100 IDX (CME)	18.54	21/06/1999	25/07/2003
E-Mini S&P 500 (CME)	-16.88	21/09/2001	25/07/2003
Euribor 3M (LIFFE)	15.04	20/04/1989	25/07/2003
Euro 100 (FTSE International)	9.02	07/05/1998	15/07/2004
Euro Bund (EUREX)	17.14	29/09/1988	25/07/2003
Euro Currency (IMM)	21.04	27/01/1984	25/07/2003
Eurodollar (IMM)	18.68	22/09/1983	25/07/2003
Euroswiss (LIFFE)	11.96	07/02/1991	25/07/2003
FTSE 100 (LIFFE)	1.16	06/07/1984	25/07/2003
FTSE 100 INDEX (FTSE International)	6.5	02/04/1984	14/07/2004
General Electric	-1.46	02/01/1962	11/11/2004
General Motors	5.4	02/01/1962	11/11/2004
Gold (COMEX)	10.76	14/04/1983	25/07/2003
Hang Seng Index (HKFE)	8.6	31/12/1986	25/07/2003
Heating Oil (NYMEX)	13.3	11/05/1984	25/07/2003
Hi Grade Copper (COMEX)	7.2	28/04/1983	25/07/2003
IBM	7.58	02/01/1962	11/11/2004
Intel	9.3	09/07/1986	11/11/2004
Japanese Bonds (TSE)	23.54	14/07/1987	25/07/2003
Japanese Yen (IMM)	21.2	28/03/1984	25/07/2003
London Copper US$ (LME)	20.4	02/01/1968	25/07/2003
Long Gilt (LIFFE)	18.74	29/12/1983	25/07/2003
McDonalds	-1.98	02/01/1970	11/11/2004
Microsoft	10.8	13/03/1986	18/06/2004
MSCI Taiwan Index (SIMEX)	24.14	09/01/1997	25/07/2003
NASDAQ	18.22	12/11/1984	18/06/2004
NASDAQ100 IDX (CME)	21.92	10/04/1996	25/07/2003
Natural Gas (NYMEX)	19.82	03/04/1990	25/07/2003
NAV DAX 30	66.2	29/05/1992	15/07/2004
NIKKEI (SIMEX)	5.72	03/09/1986	25/07/2003
S&P 500 (IMM)	-6.28	16/09/1983	25/07/2003
S&P 500 Index	13.2	22/11/1982	18/06/2004
S&P/ASX 100 (S&P's Australia Index Services)	66.2	29/05/1992	15/07/2004
Short Sterling (LIFFE)	20.46	26/01/1984	25/07/2003
SPI 200 (SFE)	11.82	04/10/1983	25/07/2003
Swiss Franc (IMM)	21.48	23/01/1984	25/07/2003
Unleaded Gas (NYMEX)	8.78	03/12/1984	25/07/2003
Wal-Mart	10.44	25/08/1972	11/11/2004
Walt Disney	11.5	02/01/1962	11/11/2004
Zinc (LME)	3.8	06/09/1984	25/07/2003
Average % Bias =	*11.4*		

You may notice that there are no results presented for property prices. This is due to the difficulty of finding reliable data. However, you will have seen in Strategy 4.8 that I am convinced property prices not only move in trends, but that they do so very strongly.

8.2 Trends have been in operation for a long time

We have seen that trends are a strong force affecting market prices, and produce an average bias of about 10%. They also apply, with amazingly few exceptions, to a very broad range of markets. But there is more: trends have one hell of a track record! They have been operating almost year in, year out, for decades.

To convince yourself, you can see that the market results I presented in Strategy 8.1 are based on long sample periods. In most cases, the analysis goes back to at least the 1980s. I would also bet that markets trended even more strongly before the sample periods, when markets were probably even less efficient.

A comparative advantage that can be tested

Like all opportunities, the fact that an idea has worked well in the past increases our confidence for the future, and this long track record increases our confidence that trends will continue for some time.

Trends are the only comparative advantage that we can verify with statistical evidence. The others that we pursue in this book, by necessity, are more subjective, and are harder to measure. Any other opportunities that are as easy to identify as trends, have been wiped out, as exploitation led to elimination.

Trend following is becoming more popular

It is not surprising then, that trends have been getting some attention from big investors. When I first tested for trends more than twenty years ago, I was not aware of any similar research. Markets then were very volatile, so there was no shortage of trading opportunities, and perhaps people didn't feel the need to do much homework. They were a bit lazier back then! In the last ten years, however, many investors have discovered the opportunity offered by trending markets. Trading in line with the trend has become extremely fashionable, especially with hedge funds. It is so well known that it has earned a mainstream title: 'momentum trading'.

The attractions of momentum trading are obvious. It's not exactly hard work - simply buy when markets are going up, and sell when they are going down. There is no sweating over the fundamentals trying to come up with original ideas. The rewards on offer are substantial. A 10% bias is a fantastic opportunity to generate long term profits. For every hundred times you back a trend, you can pocket ten more equal-sized winners than losers. In addition, because trends are so widespread across so many different markets, it is not too difficult to diversify and to reduce the volatility of the returns.

8.3 It is not true that markets usually overreact

Whenever a market goes a long way, people trot out the old chestnut that 'markets always overreact'. It's a common and widely held belief; almost a mantra.

Most traders believe that the market overreacts. "Just look at the tech market or even the South Sea Bubble", they say, usually with a smug look. But don't be misled. At any given time, the market is more likely to continue in the direction it has been travelling, rather than swing around and go back the other way. The fact that markets trend, mean that they generally take time to reach their destination. The truth is, most of the time market prices are in transit.

I can think of far more examples of markets making big, slow moves to reach the right level, than tech wrecks or South Sea Bubbles.

- Think of the Dow Jones over the last 25 years. There, the 1987 stock market crash looks like an aberration rather than a correction.
- Think of the dollar-yen exchange rate falling from around 400 to nearly 100.
- Think of the big falls in interest rates around the world in the last 25 years.

In these cases, which are far more typical, the market spent the vast majority of the time slowly moving in the right direction. If there was an inefficiency in the market, it was that the market went too slowly and under reacted.

My reasoning is very significant to investors because of its implication: *don't look for opportunities where the market's going to reverse, look for those where it's going to continue on its path.* This is the subject of a later Strategy.

8.4 Trends are resistant despite being well-known

Trends can provide a significant opportunity for investors. By backing the trend, you get a few percentage points of probability in your favour.

Most opportunities like these in the financial markets are pretty well wiped out soon after they are discovered. If you find a cheap place to buy apples and can sell them for a profit to your local greengrocer, you'll buy them all until there's none left. It's the same effect in the markets. Exploitation leads to elimination.

However, trends are resilient. Because they only provide a few percentage points advantage, they are not as obvious or as easy to exploit as cheap apples.

The phenomena of trends will survive

Even though they are very well-known, I believe that trends will be one of the last survivors of market inefficiencies. Trends are protected by the huge forces behind them. They are not caused by some simple error in pricing, but rather by some big fundamentals that are very enduring and not easily eliminated. In the next few Strategies, I am going to briefly discuss the causes of trends:

- information is absorbed gradually by the market;
- price changes are slowed by inertia and scepticism;
- rising prices attract buyers; and
- economic cycles breed market cycles.

It is very important to understand these forces affecting price behaviour. An observation - such that prices move in trends - is far more powerful when the reasons behind it can be identified and understood.

8.5 Trends represent the gradual dispersal of information

I always try to understand why an opportunity exists. If I can be sure of the reasons, I am more certain that I am not missing something, and it makes me more aware of how long the opportunity will last. Later we will see that I use trends as a major part of my trading technique by combining them with my view on the fundamentals. So it is important for me not to just be satisfied that trends exist, but to also understand what causes the trends.

The first cause of trends that I have identified is that the full implications of important information are not immediately absorbed by all of the market.

What does the news really mean?

It may be surprising to think that markets are slow to fully appreciate new information. In this day and age, a steady flow of statistics and announcements is spread by lightning-fast communications and produces instantaneous reactions.

The knee-jerk response by the market however is not the whole story. The *implications* of the news are often subtle and can require more time to be fully absorbed by the price.

What if there's no monthly announcement?

Big picture developments in the economy and society, such as the steady rise of China, are often underestimated by markets. They do not get the same burst of attention and news coverage as the monthly numbers. So even though China is very important to the markets, its influence cannot be summarised by one statistic, and market participants react to it at their own pace.

To summarise this Strategy, information and analysis can take time to be dispersed through the market place. This delay in reactions causes prices to trend.

> Information and analysis can take time to be dispersed through the market place.

8.6 Price reaction is delayed by inertia and scepticism

It is human nature to persist with our views even with the appearance of new compelling evidence to the contrary. This shows up in market prices as well. Sometimes big moves in prices are completely justified when new information becomes available. The reason they don't happen immediately is that some people take time to be convinced. This slows down the process so that you get a trend towards the right price, rather than an instantaneous adjustment.

In the early 1990s, there was strong downward pressure on inflation and interest rates, but there were still many sceptics, especially following the inflation-ridden 1980s. I seem to remember even Alan Greenspan took time to be converted. Didn't he fret that rising gold prices in the mid 1990s would signal coming inflation? Something he may be embarrassed about now, especially since he seems to get the credit for the low interest rates we have today. Anyway, bond rates took their time coming down, and in general, a nice trend developed.

Herd instinct slows re-evaluation of forecasts

The strong herd instinct among analysts and economists helps to sustain the inertia. Apart from a very small number who seek the resulting notoriety, few forecasters like to risk their reputation by making a 'big call'. It is far easier for them to lose credibility than it is to gain it. Few people would have been brave enough to predict the NASDAQ nearly doubling in 1999, or indeed to predict it dropping by nearly eighty per cent soon after. Consequently, everyone adjusts their expectations about fundamentals and prices quite slowly, and the slower reaction results in trends.

8.7 A rising price attracts buyers

In economic theory, rising prices reduce demand, and falling prices increase demand. Think of apples. If apple prices rise, people naturally buy fewer of them and choose something else. On the other hand, if apple prices fall, people will buy more of them.

Our humble apple is a fairly straightforward asset. It is bought to be eaten and there is no guessing about its future. Its price is fairly constant and any movement is fairly easy to explain.

In the financial markets however, it can be very different. *Rising prices may actually attract buyers, and falling prices may attract sellers.*

It's all about the future

In many cases, the buyer of a financial asset is taking a view about its future price. Unlike apples, these assets have no simple intrinsic value. You can't eat your share certificate! Financial assets are bought to provide some sort of financial gain. In general, the buyer needs the confidence that eventually, someone else will be willing to buy the asset from them at a reasonable price.

However, it is difficult for investors to be very confident about the future. Markets are bombarded with information, and it is a challenge to find any coherent message from all of the different facts and rumours. Because of these difficulties, psychology plays a big role in the markets.

Psychology

Because valuing financial assets is extremely difficult, we are very much influenced by how others see them. When we see a price starting to move higher, far from being deterred by the higher price, it is in fact easy to be tempted to buy. It is completely natural to do the following:

- Extrapolate and assume the market will go even higher.

- Feel that since others are buying, it must be a good idea. Those buyers are probably 'in the know'.

- Feel emboldened as a buyer, because you are not alone.

It can be surprising to outsiders to discover that finance is not all about logic and mathematics! This kind of behaviour affects both professionals and amateurs. Rising prices attract more buying and falling prices more selling. This is one of the ways markets move in trends.

8.8 Economic cycles breed market cycles

The economy moves in cycles. It doesn't tend to heat up and cool down at random. Even with the nice expansion of the global economy in the last 25 years or so, there have been several well-defined mini cycles.

Now most, if not all, market prices are largely affected by the state of the economy. So, prices as well have a tendency to move in cycles. Even those markets that look way into the future, such as long term interest rates, currencies and stock prices, are greatly affected by the cycle, and so they reflect the cyclical pattern.

In a perfectly efficient market, the economic cycle would be well anticipated. After all, doesn't the economy usually bounce back from a recession? However, as with other big picture influences, analysts take time to be convinced. That is why in Chapter 5, I have suggested using a big picture view of the economy as a guide for investing in the different market sectors.

8.9 News against the trend is often ignored

Early in my career, I was already keeping a rough idea of whether markets I followed were in an up-trend, down-trend or non-trend. I started to watch their behaviour with this in mind. It became clear to me over time that the trend of a market affected its reaction to news.

Time and time again I noticed how often up-trending markets ignore bad news.

Look at history to understand how markets have behaved to specific events in the past

Years ago, I did some research on how Australian interest rates responded to news announcements. In those days, the monthly employment figure was vital. The number of jobs that the economy gained or lost was a big influence on the bond market.

So we looked back at the data to see how many points the bond price moved for every 10,000 jobs difference between the expected and the actual announcement. To do this, we compared the prices just before the announcement, to the prices at various times afterwards.

My interest then, was to see how stable the relationship had been, and, if possible, to use it to take positions.

With the information, on an announcement I had a target for where the market was going, and I could take a position if the price moved slowly enough. If an announcement implied that the bond market could rally by 12 basis points over the next few days, and after ten minutes it had only rallied 6 points, I could jump in and buy.

This technique would involve some short term trading, which I usually don't endorse. However, it was based on a proven relationship, and no one else in the market at that time was doing that kind of analysis. So there was a logical reason it could work. I guess it was also a twist on the idea that markets take time to react.

Market response to news is dependent on the prevailing trend

It was in the course of this analysis, that we confirmed a long held belief. We found that the response of the market was very different depending on whether there was an up-trend or down-trend at the time of the announcement.

Upward trending markets are more likely to ignore bad news, and get a better boost from good news.

This is further proof of the power of the trend. In theory, markets should not do this. Previous price moves are not supposed to have any bearing on future price moves. The Strategy here gives us more confidence when, in the next chapter, we combine trending behaviour with a fundamental viewpoint.

9 | Market Timing

9.0 Combine fundamentals with price action

The analysis in the earlier chapters has been very important. You need these winning ideas to make money in the markets. However, you also need to implement the winning ideas effectively. I have met many people who have good ideas, but lousy implementation brings them unstuck. They have bad habits like buying into falling markets or cutting their good positions too early. As with many things, 'timing is everything'. There is nothing more frustrating than being right about the market, but somehow in the end, losing money.

In this chapter, I am going to present to you a very powerful trading technique that is backed up by logic and experience. The technique involves using the bullish or bearish view that is derived from the fundamentals, and combining it with the price action to increase its effectiveness.

Trading rules

The method is as follows:

Before investing

1. A view is formed on a market using the fundamentals.
2. A decision is made on the size of the investment, and on a stop-loss level.

Entry

1. The investment is only made when a trend develops in the right direction. There is no attempt to get a bargain in a falling market.
2. If the investment then becomes unprofitable, the position is not increased. There is no attempt to 'average down'.

Exit

1. The position is finally cut if the price deteriorates to the stop-loss level (alternatively, the stop-loss level may be moved if: the reasons for the price move are thoroughly understood and the loss is not threatening to be destructive), or

2. the fundamentals change for the worse, or

3. the trend finally reverses.

Note that even if your view becomes well-known and part of a consensus view, it is not a reason to cut a position. In fact, I will argue later that being with the consensus can be a good thing. Similarly, no price target or time limit is used for cutting a winning position.

Two successful trading styles combined into one

The biggest price moves will occur when the fundamentals and the price direction are in agreement. At various times over the past fifteen years, I have designed and successfully used trading models that are based purely on price. In these models, no consideration was given to any fundamental information, and yet they were extremely profitable. I believe that although it is more difficult, fundamental trading can be even more successful. The idea is to put two successful trading styles into one. The result can be astounding.

9.1 Ignore the noise in price movements

I was once sitting with a trader who had a big position in the dollar-yen market. Unfortunately, the position was well underwater and it was hurting. The trader was talking to the currency brokers every few minutes, and demanding to know why the price had moved up or down by a few points. The stress was tough for him, and he wanted my help. My response was to ensure firstly, that he was still confident on his fundamental view, and secondly, that he had a stop-loss in mind if the market kept moving against him. Having done that, the next thing I advised was that he really must forget about the small up and down moves. They are nothing more than static on a radio.

There will always be small moves in the market, which are not driven by any fundamentals. This 'noise' is often caused by just a few buyers or sellers in the market.

Noise is meaningless.

Decide what is the trend direction

On the other hand, we would like to have a feel for the trend direction of the market. The trend gives us some inkling of what is statistically likely to happen in the future, and we want to use that information for our trading decisions. So we need to decide at what point a price move is meaningful enough to be considered a trend.

I have mentioned earlier in the book that a trend probably requires a move of at least five, or even ten percent, but to trust your instincts. In general terms, I can give the following advice.

For the bigger markets, such as currencies, blue chip stocks, and property, I have usually considered a 5% move a significant move. So if the pound rises fairly smoothly against the dollar, from say $1.80 to $1.89, I would be happy to say that it was a true uptrend and not just noise.

Smaller markets are more effected by random buying or selling than the bigger markets, so for those you need bigger moves to be confident that it is more than noise. A trend for a medium sized company may require a move of at least 10%, and for a small company it could be at least 20%.

With your view on the trend direction you should endeavour to *buy a rising market, sell a falling market.* This will guide us with our market timing as we implement our views from the fundamentals.

9.2 Don't be a hero - do not buy falling markets

The first step towards putting on a trading position is to avoid the mistake of getting in too early. It is a great feeling to buy into a weak market that you think has gone too far, and then watch it nicely recover. You feel very clever and like a hero, since you spotted an opportunity that others missed, and your timing was brilliant. However, I think it is too difficult to rely on this technique.

Never forget: markets move further than expected and they move in trends

Trying to predict a turn in the market – unless there is clear panic situation – is logically inconsistent with my beliefs on the markets, for two reasons:

1. We have seen that I believe markets are often surprising us by moving further than expected. We are therefore likely to badly misjudge where we think the market will bottom out.

2. I have also presented statistical proof that markets move in trends. Consequently, probability suggests that when they are falling, they are more likely to continue to fall, than to suddenly reverse direction.

These two pieces of logic are fundamental to my Strategies, and part of the reason I have thoroughly presented my arguments that the markets move a long way and follow trends.

I was fortunate enough to come to these conclusions early in my trading career, and they have saved me a hell of lot of money. Many, many times I have really felt like buying into a market that looked cheap, and I have been disciplined enough to hold back. Time and time again, I have then seen the market carry on further and I have realised I could have made a costly mistake. I would have been lucky to pick the low, say, 1 time in 10. If I had backed intuition rather than logic, my trading career would have been very short indeed.

Fighting the trend is for mugs

I have seen many good traders come unstuck by trying to be a hero. They may have thought that being a 'contrarian' is clever and gutsy. I argued in Chapter 1 that we should 'fear the market', and hence my view is that in most cases, fighting the trend is simply futile.

9.3 Trade with the trend - wait for the trend before you enter the market

In the earlier chapters I have discussed various themes to be used to generate investment and trading ideas:

- there remain patterns and anomalies in the markets;
- markets are slow to react to structural influences; and
- that small companies offer the best opportunities on the share market.

However, before investing, we should wait for the market to give some confirmation of our viewpoint. Once the price does start moving in the correct direction, it is a signal that our view on the fundamentals could be the right one, because other people are starting to form the same opinion.

Therefore, when we want to enter a market, the idea is to wait for a price trend in the right direction.

One of the most important Strategies

This is one of the most important Strategies and it has worked well for me time and time again. On one occasion a few years ago, I decided to sell some US dollars that I had held for a number of years, and to switch into euros. My decision was based on some familiar big picture influences in the US: weakening economic growth, falling interest rates and ballooning deficits.

Meanwhile the euro had been having a bad run against the dollar, and the price had fallen to $0.95 from over $1.00. So I didn't rush. I waited and the market went far further than I expected as it fell to around $0.83. Only after an uptrend started with a bounce to around $0.88 did I buy my euros. By waiting for the trend, I avoided getting in too early and saved the difference between $0.95 and $0.88, nearly 10% of the price. It ended up being a great trade as I was able to exit above $1.20.

The logic in waiting for a trend is that it is too risky to buy into a falling market. We know that a falling market has more chance of falling further, than it has of rebounding. On the other hand, once a market starts to rise, it has more chance of rising further, than of falling back.

9.4 Add to winning trades, not losing trades

Somehow, this Strategy became instinctive to me well before I knew of any logic behind it. I guess it had something to do with being a slightly nervous trader in the early days. I didn't want to add to losing positions, because I feared I was just compounding a mistake. On the other hand, having some paper profit on a winning position gave me the confidence and the protection to add to it.

Ruining markets

Twice in my career, I have been accused of "ruining" a market. The first was in the early 1980s at Bankers Trust, when we spotted an opportunity to quote long-dated Australian dollar prices to clients.

Occasionally, customers needed to be able to buy and sell dollars for settlement up to ten years in the future. The only market makers were the four existing Australian banks, and their prices were very expensive. It was difficult for the banks, because deals were done very infrequently, and it was not easy for them to match buyers with sellers.

However, I figured out how to derive the prices from other, more liquid markets, and I was able to offer dramatically better prices to customers. This didn't make one banker from the big four very happy, so he telephoned and told me, angrily, that I was "ruining it". I wasn't too rattled since I figured we must be winning a lot of business from our competitors!

The second occasion was when I learnt the art of adding to winning positions. It was the beginning of my trading career and I had started to trade my first market, Australian interest rates. This time, I copped it from one of my colleagues in another area of our dealing room. For years he had been quietly trading interest rate futures, and making small returns by catching intra-day moves of 0.1% here and there. I ruined it for him, he said, when I started doing big volumes and pushing the price around. In a way, though, my influence was just an inevitable step towards the market becoming more efficient.

My big picture view was that Australian rates were on the way up, and I was being proved right. It was early in 1988 and the central bank was making a reassessment. Fearing a recession, they had responded to the 1987 share market crash a few months earlier, by cutting interest rates.

However, paradoxically, the economy actually stayed too strong and started to overheat. "The champagne glass is bubbling over", is how the Treasurer, Paul Keating, so nicely described it. So interest rates were on the way up.

And up they went. I am not talking about small moves of 0.1% here or there. This was the start of a big trend, and from March 1988 to June 1989, short term rates rose hundreds of points: from around 11% to over 18%.

I got onto this move early. Unlike my mate in the dealing room, I didn't grab the first profit I saw. I did the opposite, and added to my winning position. I was very convinced about the fundamentals pushing rates higher, and I did not want to lose the opportunity. So over a period of months I aggressively accumulated a big futures position which caused some movement in the market. As a trader, even a green one, I wanted to get a big position on. I knew that prices were not coming back to these levels for a long time.

It ended up being one of my most satisfying trades, which made us close to $20 million. It was a huge amount for a small bank at that time. The win kick-started my trading career, and in the following year I was put in charge of the new trading department. Just as important was what I had learnt. What started as instinct has become a habit: *add to winning trades when the fundamentals look good.*

Don't add to losing trades

What about adding to losing trades? Surely if you bought something at a 100, it is a good idea to buy a few more if the price drops to 90? However, I don't agree, and I have never done it.

My logic is consistent: respect the market, protect your capital, prices move in trends and the market goes further than expected. All of these are inconsistent with adding to losing trades. The times it works, will not pay for the times it does not.

Cutting losing positions

Far from adding to losing positions, you should keep an eye on your stop-loss levels. We have talked about stop-losses, and my recommendation has been to:

1. have a stop loss in your mind when you make an investment; and
2. if the price hits the stop-loss level, make a judgement on whether to cut.

The judgement depends on your confidence about the fundamentals at the time, and your ability to handle further losses if the price deteriorates even more.

9.5 It is safe to be with the consensus

I was sitting in a London pub with some bankers, when I was asked for my view on a market, and my comment was that I agreed with the consensus view. I could immediately tell from the look on one fellow's face, that he thought I was totally naïve, or even worse. "The consensus is always *wrong!*", he spluttered.

I definitely do not agree. In fact, *if you want to be onto a big move in the markets, at some point you will need the consensus to be with you.*

As you know, I don't trust the experts in the media to outguess a market price. However, this does not mean that they cannot reflect a broad consensus on the fundamentals. After holding a position for a while, the reasons for your position may become well-known and obvious. In fact, you may put on a position when these things are already well-known. These fundamentals can continue to drive the price even when they are broadly discussed and receiving a lot of attention.

Most big trends have involved long periods where the driving influences seemed obvious and well-known.

1990s fall of the Japanese stock market

A good example was the decline in the Japanese stock market. At the beginning of 1990, the Nikkei was close to 40,000 and by 2003, it had fallen to 7,500 before it bounced to about 11,000 today. What is amazing is that most of the factors pushing it down were widely known at the beginning of the market slide. In particular, there was the weak banking sector and weak economic growth. These fundamentals were the consensus for a long, long time.

Strong oil prices

Another example is the oil price. I have discussed oil earlier, and over the last couple of years it has seen a strong price rise with a tripling in price. Some of the reasons driving it higher have been pretty much the same for much of that period. They included the tensions in the Middle East, instability in Nigeria and the steady increase in demand from China and the rest of Asia. Now, none of these were particularly new, and they were all quite well-known.

When markets experience these big moves, they can attract an increasing amount of media coverage and analysis. If you have a position that is doing well, this attention can make you nervous. You may be tempted to think that all of the news is already in the price. Don't be concerned, it is safe to be with the consensus, and there is no other way to stay on a big move.

9.6 Do not use price targets or time limits

In February 2000, I became keen on an unlisted UK company called Amino Technologies. These guys design and make 'set top boxes' - the boxes that sit on a TV and deliver cable and other TV services. The company's strength is in the price competitiveness of their products, and some software innovation. When the company was private, I built up an investment with an average price of under 50p. It floated on the market in mid 2004 with an opening price of over 130p, and I was, of course, very pleased. Over the next few months, it went even higher to 175p, and I sold some of my position.

This was a mistake, because I broke my own rules. I was very bullish on the fundamentals and I had some silly notion that the market could go to 200p over twelve months. I then felt that because it had almost reached that target so quickly, it was time to sell. It wasn't! The trend continued, and the price later soared to 300p.

The lesson from this example is: do not use price targets. I don't know why I did. I had recommended the stock to friends, who naturally asked how far the price could go, and I had given 200p as a guide. The problem with targets is that the price goes further than expected (Strategy 7.0). I formed the target when the price was 130p, so when it neared 200p so quickly, it was very tempting to sell. However, more people were becoming aware of the bullish story on the stock, and the price move showed that they were starting to be convinced.

The winners have to outbalance the losers

You might be wondering, 'What's he whinging about, he made a great profit?'. Fair enough, I did. But I make losses too. It is vital to manage your winning positions and to try to make the most from them. If you do this well, you can back some very big winners, which will help you to survive the inevitable losses.

Using targets shows a belief that you can correctly value a financial asset. The wild swings in the markets over the last hundred years show that finding a correct price for something is extremely difficult or even impossible.

Time limits on investments should be unnecessary

In this Strategy, I have also warned about using time limits. I have given this a lot of thought. What if you make an investment because the market fundamentals look good and the price has been trending higher, but then nothing much happens? Should you give up on the idea? Certainly, if it's an expensive position to hold because you are paying funding costs, you should consider cutting. Otherwise, I don't want to impose an arbitrary time limit. It is particularly important to allow a lot of time for big picture trades, because the markets can be very slow to react to structural changes in the economy and society. On other, more specific types of trades, I have found it rare that nothing happens over a long period. Either the fundamentals change, leading me to give up on the idea, or the price gets going.

The time to get out is when the trend reverses

In summary, a reliable way to exit a winning position with good fundamentals is to allow the price trend to finish. This demonstrates that the idea has run its course. The price reaching an arbitrary target or a period of time elapsing, is not a reliable signal. I will explain more later. First, though, a warning is given in the next Strategy: even if a trade is doing well, keep an eye on those fundamentals.

9.7 If the fundamentals have changed, adjust the position accordingly

In the heady days of the recent tech bubble, investors were clamouring to jump on the bandwagon. Just about any early-stage tech company could raise money at a very high valuation. All of them were promoted as a potential Intel, so they had to be worth a fortune!

The world had not always been so crazy. Traditionally, the rough way to get valuations is to use a price-earnings ratio, which can make a lot of sense. Using earnings, or loosely speaking, profits, provides a benchmark for company values.

Most of us are familiar with the idea. For example, if the ratio implied by market prices for a particular sector is 8, and a company makes profits of $1 million a year, you would expect the company to be valued at about $8 million. The share price would be simply $8 million divided by the number of shares in issue. In that way, the company is on a par with others in the same sector, although it may have a higher or lower valuation if it has special positive or negative features.

How to value growth oriented tech companies?

The problem with this methodology for new tech companies was that during the tech craze, most of them did not have any profits. So a price-earnings ratio wouldn't work. However, frenzied investors were not too worried about company profits. Dominating a world market was far more important. Profits could even signal that management was not being aggressive enough, and would lose out to a competitor that was more growth oriented.

So investors started to look at sales revenue. The tech companies would often have sales, even if they did not have profits. Consequently, the companies could be valued by using a price-revenue multiple, and a number around ten was often used. This worked as a guide, until later in the boom. As the bubble grew bigger and bigger, more and more companies raised money, not just with an absence of profits, but also with an absence of sales.

How do you value something that may just be a bunch of people with an idea? That's all that some of these companies were, and they were raising big money.

A rough rule of thumb, quoted to me during the boom, was that a company could be valued at $2 million per engineer. A 'price-engineer ratio' I guess! That is when I really became nervous about the crazy valuations in the tech sector. There was no way that I would believe that a company that does nothing more than hire 10 engineers is suddenly worth $20 million! And I like engineers, my brother Peter is one.

As well as engineers, web page designers were in big demand. Around this time I met someone who had designed a beautiful series of web pages. He had some contacts and wanted to start an internet service provider. His artwork was the first step, and he had spent about three months on its design. He wanted to raise £4 million, and the new company would be valued at £5 million. In other words, his artwork was to be valued at £1 million – more than some Picasso paintings!

The fundamentals had changed

I didn't invest in this or just about any other tech company in the final twelve months of the boom, and I tried where I could, to sell my tech investments. I had been investing in tech since 1995, but, to me, the fundamentals of the tech sector had changed. The quality of new tech companies had dropped tremendously, and they were being funded with a lot of cheap money from naïve investors.

This was my decision despite the fact that share prices in the tech sector were trending straight upwards and that decision saved me a hell of a lot of money when the crash came.

The tech crash is a great example of where fundamentals are the most important consideration, and where the trend may not be your friend. The strategy here is to monitor the fundamentals, and to cut positions accordingly, even if the trend is still in your favour.

9.8 You will not get the high or the low

In the early 1990s, the Bankers Trust Australia dealing room had taken one of its biggest market positions ever. My department and a number of others had a strong view on Australian interest rates, which was that they would continue to fall. The position was a good one, and the profits were already substantial. On one particular day, when I recall the central bank cut official interest rates by more than the market expected, the bond market price shot up in our favour. The paper profit on that morning alone was over $10 million.

A slot machine trade

We were all obviously ecstatic. It is a great adrenaline rush when all of your analysis and risk-taking proves so well-founded. The prices on the screen were going higher and higher, as fast as coins dropping out of a slot machine. There was a buzz around the dealing room with everyone talking at once, and even the people not directly involved had become keen spectators.

However, the senior management of the bank were nervous about the big position. They were anxious to lock-in the big win.

So I was appointed the task of deciding when to cut and take profits for all of the departments.

Management had wanted to cut as early as ten million, but I held on and our paper profit peaked at seventeen million. I then cut the position when it pulled back to fifteen million. To me, we were five million better off, but I will never forget their reaction to the fifteen million figure: "Well done. But shame we just lost two million."

You've got to laugh, right?

Always leave some money on the table

The way that I trade, I will never have the satisfaction of getting the best price or the biggest possible profit. I always use this technique: if the fundamentals remain the same, *wait for the trend to turn, before getting out of a winning position.*

In this way, I will never get the high or the low, because I will wait for a reversal before I exit.

I would not have been confident that the Australian bonds on that day would move as far as they did, and it would have been easy to cut too early. Ten million looked like a high, and so did twelve million. By waiting for a reversal, we pocketed fifteen.

The exit technique is logically consistent with the entry technique because both use the price to dictate the best timing. Again, they are both based on the belief that markets trend and surprise us by how far they go.

9.9 A powerful model shows probability is on your side

I once made about a million dollars out of a hobby. It obviously was not tennis, skiing or chess, but my trading model, Trend Trader. It was the second half of the 1990s. I was living in Monte Carlo and my main activity was investing in small companies and trading other markets.

For a few minutes each day, I updated the model on my laptop, using the daily open-high-low-close prices. I would then send the market orders to my broker. Trend Trader was trading ten markets, and it was fun to watch, even when it differed from my own trading.

During that time, I travelled to some fantastic places. One was the bush blocks of Sierra Leone, where I had been crazy enough to buy a small diamond mine. For that trip, I took a satellite phone, so I could keep in touch with the Bloomberg system and send the orders. Sitting on a tree stump juggling a satellite phone in one hand and a laptop computer in the other, sure fascinated the locals!

As time went by, I became too busy with other things, and I stopped trading the model and banked my profits.

You may recall that I designed Trend Trader when I was at Bankers Trust in the late 1980s. We enjoyed great success with it, by trading many different markets around the clock. This required a team of four or five and sophisticated programs to monitor our positions. Years after I left, they were still using it, and in one of those years, I was told that it was the biggest earner in the trading room. Sadly, they never sent me a royalty cheque!

Trend Trader has worked in theory and practice

Earlier in this book, I explained how years ago, I first ran Trend Trader on historical data. The results, which stunned me, confirmed that over long periods, most markets moved in trends. By backing the trend with equal-sized bets, you were a winner 55% of the time, and a loser only 45% of the time.

The practical results achieved over the years with Trend Trader have firmly backed up these theoretical results. It is always pleasing when things dreamt up in the 'lab', work in the real world. You get the reassurance that there's nothing amiss with the Petri dish!

Our trading style mimics Trend Trader

Trend Trader is based on the theme of markets moving in trends. It basically works like this:

1. Wait for a price trend to develop, and buy or sell in line with the trend.

2. Keep the position and only cut if the trend is broken by a meaningful reversal.

You may recognise that Trend Trader is consistent with what I have recommended in this chapter to use as a trading style: wait for an underlying trend before entering the market, and wait for a turn before exiting. The success of the trading model, which does not use any fundamental viewpoint at all, gives us comfort that our trading style is sound.

But we can do even better...

Our trading can be even more powerful than Trend Trader. The model blindly buys and sells as the price changes. It has no interest in the fundamentals.

But we can use our view on the fundamentals to our benefit.

We will still *buy a rising market, sell a falling market*, but we will be led primarily by our views on the world. *If our own analysis of the fundamentals is any good, we should outperform the model.*

I have discussed a host of ways to analyse the fundamentals, which include:

- ignore the experts;
- look for patterns and anomalies;
- examine big picture changes;
- choose the right markets; and
- consider small companies.

I believe that these are very powerful techniques.

So by imitating its disciplined trading style, and adding a touch of flair, we have a real chance of doing even better than Trend Trader. That would be very good indeed.

10 | Avoiding Temptation

10.0 Know when to stay out of the market

Over the years, I have noticed that we all have a tendency to think that there are opportunities in the markets, even when we shouldn't. It becomes part of a mindset. You think your job is as a trader, and you start each day with the assumption that there are some good trades out there. I used to find it particularly hard when I was working for other people because I always felt a need to justify my salary. Even now, investing for myself, I feel I need to put my capital to work to earn a return, especially since passively leaving funds in a bank deposit does not pay very well.

Sometimes the best trade is no trade at all

The fact is, that sometimes the best trade is no trade at all. I admire people who are avid risk-takers, but who are disciplined enough to stay out of the markets when there are no opportunities. This ability, I feel, separates the good traders from the very good traders.

Sometimes the markets are just quiet. The fundamentals are stable and there are no price trends. These periods are quite obvious and shouldn't tempt us into taking a position.

It is more dangerous for traders when the fundamentals are confusing, and prices are volatile. This is when I have seen many people get too convinced by one point of view, and take on low quality positions.

US dollar fundamentals are currently confusing

An example of this could be the US dollar.

Currently, there are strong arguments for both a stronger dollar and a weaker dollar. On the upside, there is the strengthening US economy and rising interest rates. On the downside, there is the massive US trade deficit which means that every single trading day in the foreign exchange market, there are a lot of dollars - more than one billion - for sale to foreign investors. Both stories are convincing, and when the price heads upwards or downwards it looks like, finally, one story is going to dominate.

These situations are very tricky though, and recently the price has had some dramatic moves in both directions. Anyone who has been too committed to a bullish or a bearish view has lost money.

Be careful at the end of long trends

Another dangerous time in the markets is after the end of a long trend. The fundamentals that caused the trend may have been assessed and fully absorbed by the markets, and, until there are new strong influences, it is hard to have a view. The NASDAQ had a massive fall of nearly 80% starting in 2000 and then recovered a quarter of that move in 2002 and 2003. The price fall was consistent with the fundamentals, and the downtrend was a great trading opportunity, but it is difficult to judge the strength of the bounce after such a fall.

These 100 Strategies gives some protection against these types of situations. The checklist approach should ensure that we analyse the fundamentals in a balanced way. Waiting for a supportive trend before we enter a market should protect us from most occasions when the market is just driven by noise, or is not in line with our view of the fundamentals.

Wait for a great trade to come along

There is of course, still some subjectivity, and it is vital not to lower your standards by slipping into low quality bets. Look back at your past winning trades, where you felt your assessment of the market was spot-on. Try to set that as some sort of benchmark for your current ideas. Never take a trade just for the sake of trading. Wait for something excellent to come along. There has been no absence of volatility in any of the markets in the past hundred years. Even in just the last 25, we have had booms and recessions, the tech bubble, a massive drop in interest rates, the worst terrorist attack on American soil and huge government surpluses and deficits. Be patient – there are other great trades just around the corner!

10.1 Identify what is difficult about the existing environment; It may change

In 2003, the stock market staged a good recovery. In January, the Dow was nearly 9,000; by March it fell to 7,400 before it bounced back to well over 10,000 by year's end. The turning point in March was the invasion of Iraq.

This rally has really made an impression on me. Before the war there were many worries in the markets and, of course, elsewhere about a tapestry of horror scenarios: Saddam's weapons of mass destruction, millions of suffering refugees, a broader Arab war involving Israel, terrorist attacks in the west and a war that went on without end. Who would want to buy stocks at normal prices in this environment? So the prices fell sharply to balance the risks.

The market took a long time to assimilate what happened in Iraq

As it turned out, it was a very quick war. Handling the peace has proved a bigger challenge. But none of the absolute horror scenarios were played out. What was interesting about the market at that time, was the time it took to respond to the good news.

If you wanted to buy stocks, there was a great opportunity in the days and weeks following the invasion. You did not have to buy before the war and risk the horror scenarios. By waiting for the war's end, there was a profitable trade of 2,000 points, by following a pretty smooth trend for the rest of the year.

This is a great example of the market being slow to react to the removal of difficult fundamentals. I have seen it many times in my career. The checklist approach that I have recommended is particularly good for highlighting these occurrences.

10.2 Monitoring trends may alert you to opportunities you wouldn't normally find

One plan I have toyed with is to monitor trends by using Trend Trader. The model could be automated to monitor, on a real-time basis, just about every market in the world. So, rather than using it as a trading model, I would simply use it to identify any market where there was a significant price move.

The idea is, that I would then investigate those markets and see if there was a convincing fundamental argument in line with the trend. In this way, I would use trends to alert me to changes in the fundamentals.

Alerted to new markets

Can you imagine it? Up on my screen every day would pop the names of different stocks, commodities and even property indices, from all over the world. "Oh, bananas are going up. Let's go and find out why, and see if we like the fundamentals. If we do, we'll buy some banana futures."

So I could be alerted to completely new markets. I may not know anything about bananas, but I could make an effort to find out. One thing I do believe, is that all markets take time to react to big picture structural changes. With that belief, the discipline of a checklist, and the underlying trend in my favour, I may have the confidence to take a position.

This project requires a data feed from all of the markets, as well as the intention to trade just about any of them, from orange juice to gold.

Monitoring individual sectors can be done manually

On a smaller scale, I could just monitor a sector that interests me. For example, let's say I am bullish about listed property companies in Britain. These are companies listed on the stock market that invest in property. Their price should really follow the property market, but sometimes they move in line with the stock indices instead. Now perhaps the share market has sold off and dragged them down, even though the property market itself has held up quite well. That could signal an opportunity to buy good quality property stocks. However, I don't have the time to analyse in detail every single listed property company in Britain to find the good ones. So what I could do is to monitor all of their prices, and only look further into a company if its price starts to move higher. In that way, I use the market price to separate the good from the bad.

For this, I wouldn't necessarily need a trading model to tell me when a price was trending higher. If it's something like 50 companies, I could just eyeball the prices or charts, and spot the trends manually.

I believe this process of monitoring trends is very useful. I like to keep an eye on a lot of markets in this way, even if I have no experience with them.

Summary

To summarise the technique then:

- For your **preferred markets**: monitor the fundamentals, and trade in line with a supporting trend.

- For **other markets**: monitor the prices, and investigate their fundamentals only when a price trend emerges.

10.3 With success, bank some profits

The trading technique that I have outlined in these Strategies is quite clear for winning positions: if the fundamentals continue to look good and are supported by a favourable price trend, do not take profits. I now want to add one wrinkle: if you are doing particularly well, you should cut winning positions to keep a balance in your portfolio and take cash out of the market.

Learn from former billionaires

There have been some very high-profile billionaires who have gone completely bust. Often they have been very flamboyant and charismatic risk-takers. When you hear of their failure, you can't help wondering what went wrong. Was it that they just did one deal too many? Could it have been that their ego got the better of them? Why didn't they just put a lazy hundred mill on the side, in case it all went horribly wrong?

We could dismiss these questions, I guess, with the answer that if these people had thought like that, they would not have become billionaires in the first place. They probably took a lot of risks to get there, which were too bold for most people.

Always mark-to-market your positions

There are lessons though, from the rise and fall of former billionaires. These Strategies are not about taking crazy risks, and there *has* to be a sensible way of locking-in some wins. I believe that the answer is to mark-to-market. As I have mentioned earlier, the idea is to value all of your positions on the basis of the current market price. This process ignores your original entry price, and any other price along the way, such as a high or a low.

If your investments are going really well, you may find that their mark-to-market value significantly exceeds the original risk amount you had in mind. As an example, say you allocated 20% of your assets to trading, and the positions have done so well that on a mark-to-market basis, they are now worth 40% of your total assets. Here you should probably reduce your positions and bank some profits. This would even be regardless of supportive fundamentals and a trend in your favour.

Over the years there were times when I have reduced positions which were doing well and which looked good going forward. Those decisions had nothing to do with my views on their fundamentals, but were simply to take cash out of the market.

10.4 Negotiation is an art

It is true that you get what you negotiate, not what you deserve. As an investor in small companies, I have seen all sorts of twists and turns in negotiations. Bigger companies experience similar problems and, as always, the lessons are relevant to investors.

Some business negotiations are very balanced. Neither party is in a weak position, and each has many choices. For example, I usually disagree with people who think that movie stars and footballers are overpaid. Yes, they have a fantastic life and everyone envies them, but their pay is determined in an open and competitive market. They are not part of a trade union or a cartel. The employers choose to pay the stars a lot of money rather than use lesser lights who are less costly. In that way, the stars really are one in a million. It is irrelevant whether they have taken enormous risks and hardships to get there (which many have), or had it easy along the way.

Many other business negotiations however, are not so balanced. They often take some time to complete, during which time the terms of the deal can change considerably from the original discussions.

One party of the negotiation is often stronger than the other because:

1. the deal is not critical to them;
2. they have no competition for the deal; or
3. time is on their side.

The stronger party can now play it quite tough. For example, they can deliberately drag out the negotiations if the weaker party is feeling the pressure to complete as the days or months pass. In Chapter 6, I talked about how some venture capital funds prey on small companies by offering great deals, that they then drag out and alter at the last minute.

Having seen all of this behaviour, I would suggest the following strategies when in negotiation:

- **Portray strength** rather than desperation to the other party.

- Do not assume the deal is done, until it has been fully completed. Continue to **maintain a dialogue** with any other interested parties, for as long as possible.

- Be aware of the **eleventh hour squeeze**, especially if you are the weaker party.

- Give out **reinforcing signals** along the way, that you will not improve your terms.

- Try to determine how much room the other party has to **improve on their terms**.

- Be the first to **draft the contract**. There are many unsaid things in a conversation, which only come out in the detail. The party who drafts the document gets to stake the first claim.

- Have some small points you are prepared in advance to surrender, so that you can **protect the more important parts of the deal**.

- **Beware of over-enthusiastic lawyers.** Occasionally, I have done a handshake deal, only to have our respective lawyers clock up expensive hours on the phone fighting over meaningless details and implausible scenarios. In the process they have moved away from commerciality. At times, they have tried to protect me with unrealistic demands on the other side, but in the process they have nearly destroyed the goodwill and killed the deal.

10.5 The evolution of the con artist

If you decide to move away from the regular markets and invest in private and obscure schemes, you are walking into a minefield. Not surprisingly, the world is full of people who want to take your money. What has surprised me over the years, is how well the con artist has evolved to avoid extinction. There are some extremely crafty people running extremely clever schemes.

Many different cons

I have come across one couple who operate as a team. They establish friendships with other couples, and then after a few months casually mention some investment ideas. The investments are private companies, which are often in another country. It might be say, oil and gas exploration in an ex-soviet regime. It sounds very exciting, but somehow it later fails. There is not much information available, and the couple pretend that they too have lost money, and affect an air of disappointment. If they can do this well, the victims don't even know that they've been ripped off. It is then an almost perfect sting, and the friendships may even remain intact. These schemers have worked their evil more than once by being pretty fluid and moving about socially. At one point, they targeted me, but fortunately I was forewarned by friends.

Other con artists are hustlers. To gain trust, they allow a target to successfully invest a small amount into an obscure scheme. The gullible victim is then happy to invest a larger amount into the next proposition. If the hustle works well, he may even bring in a few friends, and by doing so unwittingly helps the hustler find more victims. This works all the better if the target is someone of the highest integrity. When the investment fails, the hustler moves on.

A bogus invention is another ploy. A few years ago, a friend met someone at a nightclub who claimed he had invented perpetual motion. I am no physicist, but I know that perpetual motion is regarded by some as the holy grail of physics. The inventor claimed that after falling out with an eastern European university, he was seeking money to commercialise his invention. The 'proof' was a motor that ran without any obvious power source. As ridiculous as it sounds, my friend invested and, of course, lost his money.

These con artists are very convincing, and sometimes would seem to be the least likely criminals. They have the ability to persuade you to do something ill-considered. I have lost money to a guy who was very academic, very humble and even slightly nerdy. I even met his family, who seemed very decent people. He encouraged a number of us to invest in a small listed company which he was widely promoting. He claimed it had very exciting prospects, and the price looked cheap if you believed his hype. It mysteriously went wrong, and we lost our money. It was only when the authorities started prosecuting him after complaints from another group of investors, that we realised what had happened. It appears that he had secret holdings in the company which he had been actively selling at the high prices.

Alarm bells

There are some obvious considerations before you invest money in anything slightly unusual. Don't invest:

- if something sounds too good to be true (it probably is);
- if you are pressured to put money in quickly, without a satisfactory explanation;
- if you cannot verify the person's background or integrity; or
- if it is odd that you have been approached, rather than brokers or venture capitalists.

When these alarm bells start ringing, remember: the conman is not extinct.

10.6 Wealth preservation is not simple

I used to be a little suspicious about people who inherited money and didn't do too much with their lives. Over the years, my position has completely turned, and I now admire people who inherit money and don't blow it. It's actually not that easy.

Many famous people lose their money, particularly sports people. They have no experience in business or finance and are obvious targets for people looking to take advantage of them.

People who win the lottery seem to lose their winnings incredibly quickly. I met a fellow recently who had won £1 million. He is about 30, and has no family to support. He has given up his job, bought two cars for a £100,000 each, and set up his own music studio for a quarter of a million, because he likes playing the guitar. It does sound like fun. The problem is, that he never expects to work again. This is where I would apply my 3% benchmark.

The 3% Rule

If you want to maintain your wealth in real terms, you can probably spend no more than 3% of your capital each year.

The idea is that real interest rates are generally around the 3% level. At the moment for instance, five year rates are roughly 5%, inflation is roughly 2%, and that leaves you 3%. Now you may think that you can earn more than the 5% offered by interest rates. Investing in the share market for example, has outperformed interest rates over the long term, so that could help. But by trying to do better than interest rates you will also risk losses. The share market can be volatile with long bleak periods for investors who move away from low risk investing. The other problem of course is tax. Governments are not great at giving tax allowances for inflation, so that requires some careful thought.

The fellow who won the lottery could probably have counted on earning £30,000 per year in real terms if he had invested the entire £1 million. That is probably less than his job was paying. So even though he feels rich, and all his friends want a loan, he may struggle to live off his capital. Perhaps the cars and the studio weren't such a good idea.

The era of low risk, high returns is over for the moment

The task of just maintaining wealth is a challenge for many people, not just those lucky in the lottery. After the last few decades many people became accustomed to annual low-risk returns of over ten per cent. Those days are gone and wealth preservation is more difficult.

10.7 Be sceptical of sophisticated retail products

I was sitting in an expensively decorated office overlooking Monte Carlo harbour. A retail banker was giving a sales pitch for one of his bank's products. He is a good mate of mine, so he laughed when I told him that the product was a bit dodgy. It sounded like a real winner: in five years' time, I would be guaranteed the full repayment of my investment, and hopefully better if it could be achieved. I remember thinking "wow, how many wealthy people are financially naïve enough to fall for this one?". The 'capital guarantee' sounds fantastic. But as I pointed out, all the fund manager would do is put enough of my money on deposit to repay me in five years' time, and gamble with the remainder. And for that, they would pay themselves a nice fee.

Many financial retail products depend on sleight of hand

Of course, sometimes this type of retail fund can do well. What I don't like though, is there can be a lot of documentation, but no real explanation of how the products really work and how much they cost. To many investors, the lure of a capital guarantee, for example, can sound like a miracle because they can't lose their capital. They are not aware that they are risking all of their interest income.

A common mistake by many amateur investors is to ignore the interest that they are foregoing by making their investments. The time value of money is important.

In the UK, rates are around 5%, so a two year investment has an 'opportunity cost' of around 10%. Keep that in mind before you give it up.

Also be wary of retail financial products if you don't fully understand what they are doing. How much risk are they taking, and what is the real fee structure? Of course, be sure to ask them when you can retract your money, and what the exit fees are.

The more complicated the product, the more chance to disguise fees

One of my first jobs when I started working in the financial markets in the mid 1980s was the design and pricing of swaps. Swaps can be incredibly complicated, and today they are mostly figured out with computer packages.

Large corporations often need sophisticated products such as swaps to reduce their business risks. An airline for example, may have revenues in many different currencies which they want to match somehow against the price of oil, one of their biggest expenses.

It was fun trying to figure out these types of problems. Normally it was a matter of combining together a number of standard financial parts in the right way to create an unusual hybrid.

In those days, the corporation usually didn't fully understand how the hybrid was put together so there were great opportunities for extremely profitable pricing from the bank's point of view. Some of our salesmen were very keen to take advantage of the situation. I remember being amazed when one colleague asked me to price a transaction to make a profit of one million dollars, which would have been a complete rip-off for the customer. We eventually toned it down to something more reasonable, though the customer may never have known the difference, because the more complicated the product, the more chance to disguise fees.

Many banks don't even understand these products

Sometimes even other banks didn't understand the complexities. There was one very big bank which would come to us to buy unusual products for their customers. On the same day we would be buying the standard parts from the same bank and selling them back as the repackaged hybrid, at a much higher price.

My scepticism of overly complicated products links back to these experiences. Many products offered to retail investors are just as complicated as some of the deals I was putting together. The investors, like the corporations and some of the banks, often do not have the knowledge to establish their fair value.

My view then, is that *you should not invest in these things unless you have a genuine need.* It may be more flexible for you, as well as cheaper, to structure something for yourself. For example, if you want a capital guarantee, you could keep your capital on deposit, and invest the interest.

Summary

I will sum up by saying that many retail products:

- offer an attractive sounding product by introducing **a carefully disguised element of risk**. Remember, there is no free lunch which allows you a higher than market return without added risk. Or,

- **involve hidden fees,** which means that they can be replicated more cheaply and with more flexibility by investors themselves.

10.8 Management and brokerage fees should be minimal in a passive portfolio

In the financial world there can be many ways to lose money on all sorts of fees and hidden costs. You should always try to be vigilant, particularly if you have a passive portfolio.

It seems fair that you pay for performance if you have invested in a fund which is trying to do more than just match an index. Even then, you should be careful of the size of any upfront or exit fees. But you should not have to pay much in the way of fees if you are simply investing in an index tracking fund, or keeping funds on deposit.

The bank wants fees

A friend of mine was setting up a structure with her trust. She had cash and property assets which she was trying to organise in a tax efficient manner. I was with her while she was discussing the set-up with her private banker over the phone. We had not been able to understand why he wanted her to take out a big loan to buy a property, when she had more than enough cash with them on deposit.

There was no tax benefit in setting up a loan, and there was a significant cost because of the difference between the loan rate and the deposit rate. It was a long conversation, and many times my friend said "just a moment", and covered the mouthpiece while she kept me informed of the dialogue. I kept urging her to insist that a simpler structure must make sense. I guess eventually the guy just cracked, and he said "but we won't make any fees that way!". I couldn't believe it. Here was a banker from a very respected institution, who had spent a long time trying to confuse my friend into doing something for no other reason than to pay some fees.

I had lunch with another friend recently, who had withdrawn a few thousand in cash from his private bank. They had also deducted a hefty fee. When he called them, they immediately said it was a mistake and it would be corrected. It made him wonder about previous times he had withdrawn cash but not checked his statements!

Ask for market prices

Years ago, I made a currency exchange for quite a large amount, over the phone. The rate the banker quoted me was miles away from the market level. When I mentioned I had a Bloomberg screen in front of me, he smartened up the price. Mind you, he still offered me a very bad 'forward' adjustment to the price which I needed because of a delayed settlement. I had to politely explain that as a derivatives trader, I used to calculate these adjustments myself, and that if necessary, I could teach him the correct method. He quickly gave me a better price.

Shop around

The last thing you want to do is to pay exorbitant fees when all you are doing are straightforward transactions.

Remember that when you open an account you're not getting married to the broker or banker. Don't be afraid to push for a fair deal or to switch accounts. There is often little loyalty shown or rewarded, and there are many attractive offers to tempt new customers.

10.9 Follow these strategies and be part of the hedge fund (r)evolution

The last few years have seen the rise and fall of the hedge fund. These funds, which look to profit from both rising and falling markets, are known for their quickness and innovation. Many of them are macroeconomic, and they want to trade on the big structural trends all over the world.

Hedge funds are currently the financial fashion

There is a real buzz about hedge funds as I write and they are doing very well in capturing market share. Low interest rates and mixed stock market performances has meant that there is demand for new types of investment. Good hedge funds can quickly raise a lot of money. I read one estimate that after doubling in five years, hedge funds in 2005 controlled nearly $11 trillion worldwide. That's about the size of the annual GDP of the United States! Some commentators think hedge funds will double again by 2008.

It can be a lucrative business. Usually there is a fixed management fee of around 2% as well as a performance fee of around 20%. With those sorts of percentages, in a good year a fund managing $1 billion can make an enormous profit. And they often don't have to give a refund if they lose money for investors in the following year. The worst that may happen after a bad year is some withdrawals from the fund, and some damage to the reputation.

Hedge funds are a part of natural financial evolution

I see this growth of hedge funds as part of the financial sector evolution. At Bankers Trust Australia in the early 1990s there were two profit powerhouses:

1. The **funds management** side, which had been extremely good at raising and managing investors' money. It had made a reputation by coming through the share market crash of 1987 in good shape.

2. The **dealing room**, with a lot of transactions being made for the bank's own account, rather than for external clients. It was also very successful, and the traders had worldwide reputations as clever risk-takers.

The cultures in the two areas were quite different. The dealing room was definitely seen as more cutting edge but perhaps slightly brash, while the funds management business was seen as more careful, considered and intellectual.

For my part, I always thought that funds management needed to become more like the dealing room. In my view, they needed changes such as fewer committees, faster response times, better risk controls and some smaller market positions. Not everyone agreed with me. When I started my new trading department, I presented a paper on the proposed style of trading to senior people in the bank. It was almost an early form of these 100 Strategies. It was met with a lot of criticism from some of the fund managers.

Over the years, I haven't changed my mind about how money should be managed, and it's reflected in these Strategies.

The future is hedged

Hedge funds will continue to grow, and other types of funds, such as mutual funds, will behave more and more like them.

What will happen if an increasing amount of money is managed in hedge fund style? Will there be greater and greater volatility? There is plenty of criticism around that assumes hedge funds are a bad thing. "Regulate them!" they say. But it's not necessary - the market will tame them. If hedge funds push prices too far in their search for volatility, some of them will lose money. People seem to forget this, but the funds have to exit their positions, and sharp reversals hurt them. So they will learn very quickly to be careful about how far they push markets.

Having said all of these nice things about hedge funds, I think at the moment there may be a bubble. This is because the quality of the people is very mixed. In this respect, it reminds me of the tech boom a few years ago, when any silly dotcom idea could raise money. In similar fashion, a lot of the funds may fail, some people will lose money and the excitement will drop off. But in the long run, there will be more and more hedge fund style money management. A washout may help fees become more reasonable and competitive, and may also see some of the poor quality managers leave the industry.

Your future as a hedge fund manager

What does a good hedge fund do, and why do I think financial management is evolving that way? I myself became a hedge fund manager in the early 1990s, way before it was a fashionable idea, and I think a good hedge fund should follow these 100 Strategies. In fact, this book could be a user manual for a hedge fund.

Alternatively, there is nothing to stop these hedge fund techniques being used by all investors. Quick access to information, cheap dealing prices and the ability to sell into falling markets are now available to everyone. So if you're careful, perhaps you can save yourself some fees.

All that is needed is imagination and discipline. And a nudge in the right direction – which, hopefully, this book has provided!

Index

A

Adam, Robert: 114

Addavita: 49

Amino Technologies: 173

Analysts: 4, 29-30, 41, 43, 45, 94, 103-104, 141, 144, 162-163

Apple iPod: 42

ARC International: 61

Asymmetric situations: 51-52, 142-144

Asymmetry: 50-51, 129, 144

Australian dollar: 31, 51, 80, 101, 144, 157, 170

B

Backgammon: 47

Bankers Trust Australia: 10, 23, 33, 36, 177, 195

Berger: 39-40

Bermuda: 9, 11, 36-37, 117

Black, Fischer: 147

Blunt, Anthony: 114

Bonds: 3, 4, 23, 43, 51, 54, 69-70, 75, 77, 87-88, 94-95, 101, 135, 143, 157, 178

Broadbent, Jillian: 33, 36

Brokers: 20, 41, 44-46, 86, 129, 166, 189

Buffett, Warren: 35, 48

Burn-out: 60

Business angel: 17

D

Data mining: 10, 152

Day trading: 145, 146

Diversification: 54, 56, 106

Dotcoms: 74

Dow Jones Industrial Average: 136

Due diligence: 109, 127, 131-134, 150

Duggan, Millicent: 7

E

Early-stage companies: 52, 53

Economic cycles: 5, 83, 88, 102, 160, 163

Economic growth: 32, 76, 87, 89-91, 93, 95, 97-98, 100-101, 169, 173

Economics: 10, 17, 21, 46, 51, 79, 82, 102, 140, 147, 153

Economist magazine: 78

Economists: 4, 17, 33, 43, 58, 60, 77, 83, 97, 136, 144, 162

Efficiency: 21, 22

Euro: 30, 32, 52, 78, 136, 157, 169

Experts: 2, 13, 18, 28-30, 32, 51, 69, 130, 132-133, 136, 172, 180

F

Farleigh, Keith: 8

Farleigh, Marjorie: iii, 15

Fees: 6, 29-30, 116, 191-194, 196-197

Flotation: 61, 128, 129

FTSE 100: 92, 157

Fundamentals: 2, 3, 10, 19, 27, 33, 46, 53, 65, 67, 68, 81, 83, 87-88, 97, 98, 109, 135-137, 145, 150, 159-162, 165-186

Futures: 19, 52, 99, 146, 170-171

G

Gold: 14, 54, 70, 94, 99, 136, 157, 161, 184

Good ideas: 3, 48, 50, 165

Government intervention: 25

Greenspan, Alan: 94, 161

Gulf War: 13-14, 136

H

Haigh, Gideon: 10

Hedge funds: 2, 56, 74, 84, 158, 195, 196

Hewlett Packard: 111

Hogan, Bruce: 10, 36, 61

Home House: 11, 32, 57, 114, 116, 130

Housing prices: 37, 80-81, 136

Hunches: 149-150

I

Illiquid markets: 22

Inflation: 4, 6, 13-14, 72, 76, 84, 87-89, 90, 91-103, 106, 161, 190

Information: 3, 5, 13, 18, 21, 22, 28, 29, 41, 42, 43, 44, 45, 46, 59, 60, 83, 87, 89, 91, 98, 131, 141, 146, 160, 161, 162, 164, 166, 167, 188, 197

Insider information: 42

Insurance: 41, 44, 45

Interest rates: 11, 13, 17-18, 24, 27, 31-35, 52-53, 69, 72-73, 76-79, 83-84, 93-96, 99, 101-104, 135, 140, 144, 151, 155-156, 159, 161-164, 169, 170, 171, 177, 181-182, 190

Intrinsic value: 14, 148, 162

IP2IPO: 117, 118, 119

IPOs: 45

N

O

P

T

U

W

X

Y

Z

FOLLOW US, LIKE US, EMAIL US

@HarrimanHouse

www.linkedin.com/company/harriman-house

www.facebook.com/harrimanhouse

contact@harriman-house.com

FREE EBOOK VERSION

As a buyer of the print book of Taming the Lion you can now download the eBook version free of charge to read on an eBook reader, your smartphone or your computer. Simply go to:

http://ebooks.harriman-house.com/tamingthelion

Lightning Source UK Ltd.
Milton Keynes UK
UKOW01f0313280717

306219UK00002B/175/P